WICHITA Rock & Roll 1950 - 1980

The Wichita Rock Music Project Team

Jay Price, Editor,
Harry Dobbin, Art Director
Joshua Rupp, Student Researcher,
Consulting Team:
Doug Webb, Mark Archibald,
Ron Schauf, Ron Starkel,
Jim Hill, Randy Crump,
Joe Sauer, Curtis Payne,
Eric Cale

Copyright © 2017

All rights reserved. No part of this publication may be reproduced, distributed, or transmitted in any form or by any means, including photocopying, recording, or other electronic or mechanical methods, without the prior written permission of the copyright holder.

Library of Congress Control Number: 2018936928

International Standard Book Number: 978-0-692-08367-3

Printed in the United States of America by Mennonite Press, Inc., Newton, Kansas. www.MennonitePress.com

Thank You!

In addition to the many people who contributed memories, stories, memorabilia, photographs, and ideas,
there are a handful of individuals whose gifts helped make the publishing of this book possible.
Thanks to their generosity, this story of the local music scene will be able to "rock on" in the form of the printed page.

This project is part of a larger effort to support scholarship at Wichita State University.
Proceeds from this book will go to the university's Department of History to fund future research activities.
The efforts here will allow students and faculty in years to come to put their work into print.

Thank you to

Terri & Doug Adams

Amy & Alan Banta

Lora & Don Barry

Leah & Andy Gore

WICHITA STATE
UNIVERSITY

Jr. Assembly, Courtesy Wichita State Special Collections

Rexall, Courtesy Wichita State Special Collections

Century II, Courtesy Wichita Sedgwick County Historical Museum

Dragging Douglas, Courtesy Wichita Sedgwick County Historical Museum

Wichita Rock & Roll 1950s-1980s

Acknowledgements 10

Introduction 11

Band Appendix 13

Part One:

    Chapter 1: A New Generation 15

    Chapter 2: The British Invasion Hits 21

    Chapter 3: The Grind 28

    Chapter 4: Hard Rock 33

    Chapter 5: A Generation Grows Up 39

Part Two:

    Wichita Band Gallery 44

Part Three:

    Poster Gallery 111

Acknowledgements

This definitely has been a team effort! So many people need to be thanked including Doug Adams, Mark Archibald, Russ "The Big O" Armitage, Dwayne Bailey, Vince Baker, Lander Ballard, Larry Bally, Alan Banta, Randy Barb, Clay Bastian, Bill Bean, Tom Beard, Theresa Bills, Fred and John Bonner, Shirley Breth, Mike Brittain, Kevin Brown, Tom Byrne, Gary Bussart, Bert Canova, Jay Cape, Jerry Chadic, Dan Chambers, David Chanowski, Russ Cherry, David Clothier, Tom Coleman, John Corkum, Mike Coykendall, Randy Crump, Jerry Cusick, Hal Davis, Harry Dobbin, Steve Downey, Lyndon Drew, Rick Ekum, Clay Emberson, Roger Empty, Rick Fisher, David Fleming, Bryan Forrester, Orin Friesen, Bill Garrison, Nancy Garvey, Arthur Glass, Bill Goffrier, Andy Gore, Gerald Graves, Randy Grohs, Berry Harris, Kaydee Haug, Jeff Hayton, Jim Hill, Mary Hill, Rick Hodge, Donnie Huffman, Chris Hutchens, Chris James, Jim Johnson, Jim Kincaid, Charlie King, Rick Lamb, Lash LaRue, George Laughead, Richard Leslie, Earl Long, Max and Dan Loveland, Jim Martin, Art Martinez, Lee McCroskey, Mike McRoberts, Mike Metz, Jim Meyer, Mike Moreno, Jim Moore, Marc Mourning, Charmene Nichols, Jack Oliver, Don Overstake, Curtis Payne, Craig Penny, Phil Pfister, Jeff Pickering, Steve Place, Curt Poole, Kenny Potter, John Potucek, Pat Preboth, Gary Ray, John Rogers, Linda Saffier, Don Sailing, Joe Sauer, Ron Schauf, Mark Schock, Francene Sharp, Mickey Sheaks, Mark Shelton, Randy Shike, John and Nikki Shirley, Jerry Spohn, Dave Sproul, Ron Starkel, Dee Starkey, Lynn Stephan, John Stewart, Conrad Stolze, Sandy Sullivan, Jerry Sumner, Dwain Terry, Lance Threet, Thom Tucker, Phil Uhlik, Dana Veith, Doug Walker, Bucky Walters, Jon Weaver, Doug Webb, Ruby White, Ron Williams, Steve Williams, Mike Witherspoon, Tom Wise, Jim Wood, Bill Wulschleger, and Michael Ybarra. The team also appreciates the help of those in the community who assisted with photographs and other materials including Fred Berry, Eric Cale, Ed Curiel, Jami Frazier Tracy, Michelle Enke, Mary Nelson, Dr. Lorraine Madway, Kathy Morgan Major, Hal Ottaway, Pat O'Connor, Marti Osborn, Vic Peroo, Keith Wondra, Kathy Roush, Barb McJimsey, Sharon Dondlinger, and Matt Riedl. If we have omitted a name here, please accept our apologies. So many people have shared their stories and insights that keeping up with all the contributors has become a project in itself. For example, there is simply not room here to thank all the people who contributed to the lively discussions and comments on the Wichita Rock Music History Project Facebook page, but please be assured that we could not have done this without all of you. Special thanks needs to go to Margarita's who was gracious enough to allow many, many meetings to share insights and memories.

Documenting this story has been a challenge. It began as an informal discussion of friends who met at the Wichita-Sedgwick County Historical Museum. As work progressed, so did the scale. The local rock story was a lot bigger and more complicated than anyone realized. Research included articles in The Wichita Eagle, the "Wichita Rock Music History Project" page on Facebook, and lots of informal interviews, emails, phone calls. Writing up the history and the various band biographies has been a truly collaborative effort. Through it all, Harry Dobbin's background in design and promotion made sure the final layout captured the look and spirit of the era.

With regards,

The Wichita Rock Music Project Team

Jr Assembly Conga Line, courtesy of WSU Special Collections

Wichita Airport, courtesy of WSU Special Collections

Introduction

Today, music is often private. We wear ear buds so that those around us don't hear. We listen to music while driving alone in the car or in the background while we work on something else. It is easy to search the internet and find exactly the song or music that fits our moods and our tastes, even in the early hours of the morning. Going to a club to hear a live band is a unique, special experience.

It was not very long ago, however, when listening to music was a social activity that could happen several times a week. Bands played to packed crowds. Every town had its own collection of musical groups. Some played for local dances. Others played regular club circuits. There were concerts and music contests. Here, groups played for fun, for money, for potential romance, and for the passion of the music. Some were well known locally with their regular fans. A few even made the leap to national fame. Others were able to transform their passion into a career such as being in the music store business or owning a club or managing sound systems. As time passed, a number of these youthful rebels became successful executives and professionals whose resources allowed them to fund their passion as a hobby or social activity. Others, however, now look back on those rock band days with nostalgia, seeing them as a time of glory to which nothing since could match.

The bands, venues, concerts, and events outlined here tell the story of a generation who came of age in between the 1950s and the 1980s. They were young just as rock & roll came on the scene and when Wichita went through some of its most dynamic and challenging times, including civil rights and economic change, paralleling major changes taking place across the world. While the rock music scene flourished in New York, Los Angeles, and Liverpool, it also lived on in less dynamic forms in cities across the country. In a place like Wichita, a medium sized blue-collar city in the middle of the Great Plains, youth listened to the big groups that appeared on the radio and on television. From the horn bands of the late 1950s to surf, from the British Invasion to heavy metal, from country rock to hair bands, these trends also showed up in Wichita. The rock bands of Wichita represent as vast, interconnected web of groups and musicians. Like a complicated genealogy, the story of the bands presented here shows how bands formed, only to change members or transform into new groups. When a band broke up, its members often found their way to new bands. Some groups were rivals who competed at battles of the bands. Some stayed local and others went out on tour. Some were just groups of high school kids who made a little extra money on the side. Others took the leap to become professional, complete with original music, band managers, distinctive costumes, and recording contracts.

The rock scene was more than just musicians. The 1950s, 1960s, 1970s, and 1980s saw a wide range of clubs form, each with their own set groups and fan base. Then there were the music stores that sold instruments, recording studios who created albums, and radio stations that played those albums. It was not that Wichita was particularly rock oriented, since most cities in the country supported a similar array of bands and venues. The Wichita rock story was vibrant, but typical for cities of its size. There was no particular "Wichita sound," that developed, given that most bands replayed popular music they heard on the radio or on records. As such, however, Wichita provides a window into just how widespread rock culture truly was in North America between the 1950s and 1980s.

This research project tried to identify the major rock bands and musicians who performed in Wichita between the late 1950s and middle 1980s. As part of the process, the team had to make some decisions. In general, a band had to have played in public more than once or twice to be considered. Solo musicians are discussed in both the main text and among the band biographies here but generelly did not get their own entries. The main focus was on bands that performed in Wichita, which meant that we did not cover bands that were from or played in Hutchinson, El Dorado, Wellington, or other locales unless there was a significant connection to Wichita. In some cases, the team decided to combine the story of one or more bands into a single entry, especially if the groups were made up of essentially the same performers or one band renamed itself. To make the listing manageable, the team decided to not include bands from the middle 1980s on unless most of the members were active during the 1950-1980 period. Moreover, the post 1980s era was a different music scene with different influences. It is one that is currently attracting the attention of a different group of researchers who will, hopefully, continue the work done here to explore the next generation of the local music story. Even within these parameters, however, tracking down bands and performers has been both an adventure and a challenge.

It has involved holding gatherings at Margarita's, posting articles in the newspaper, maintaining a Facebook page, researching back issues of old newspaper editions, scouring websites and YouTube entries, and managing an ever growing number of phone calls, letters, emails, interviews, and informal conversations. It has been a time consuming process. Several times, the team thought they were finishing up only to discover a whole new crop of bands and musicians and the process had to start over.

The goal was to be as thorough as possible but the team knew that some bands would get overlooked or not get the coverage they deserved. The project team regrets not being able to tell the stories of groups like Cockyfox, Desert Wind, Effigy, The John Hancock Band, Medusa, Richard Walters and the Aristocrats, Roanoke, and the Soul Kings among others. There were scores of club bands, small bands, high school and middle school bands, and others who are not listed and several that probably deserve full listings. Some were known among circles of friends, some were little more than a name, and others were exactly the opposite, such as collection of musicians who performed at the Flame on South Seneca in the early 1960s known simply as "the group." In some cases, a few names of band members were known but the story was too incomplete to create a fill entry. The team also knows that there are individuals who played with the bands listed who are not mentioned, perhaps because they played for a short time or were part of only one part of a band's story. The project team apologizes in advance for these oversights and welcomes any additional information. This book is not the end of the story. It is just the start.

There simply isn't space to cover all the musicians, bands, clubs, concerts, and stories. The project team hopes that this work inspires others to tell their stories and preserve their slice of an amazing time.

200 S. Broadway

Name	Page
A Bit Much	63
Albatross	79
Axis/Shady Oak Bombers	90
Badger	105
Balloon Warfare	95
Bandit	87
Band-O-Matic	106
Berry Harris	26, 49
Betterside	88
Bill Garrison	89
Blue House	67
Bo Mitchell & Easy Money	89
Board of Regents	81
Cats Cradle	97
Chaparrels/Solomon & the Monarchs	73
CLA	82
Common Ground	67
Crank	86
Cyrus Noble Whiskey Band	96
Daniel & the Lion's Den	62
Danny Loveland	31, 55
Dawayne Bailey	103
Denim	103
Dennis Hunt & the Hunters	48
Dewy & the Big Dogs	102
Dogs	103
Donny Overstake/Lotus	30, 76
Doug & the Inn-truders	61
Dove/Salty Oats	78
Dr. Ruth & Good Sax	109
Family Circle	68
Finnigan & Wood	84
Fuzzy Dice	109
Gandalf	88
Gentleman J & the Goodtimes	49
Hard Road	72
Harley Zurrett	84
Harry & the Bushmen	59
Haze	110
Headstone	88
Heavy	73
Image	91
Jake	94
James Brothers Band	91
Jay Walker & the Pedestrians	55
Jerico	86
Jerry Wood & the Peggs	18, 51
Kevin May and the Deconairs	110
Klyde Konnor/Tangle Brains	42, 109
Lander Ballard	74
Legacy	110
Legion	83
Likety Split	93
Lo & Behold	66
Mad Hatters	63
Magpie	71
Majestic Mood/Tin Ear	83
Mama's Pride/Syzygy	73
Manilla Road	35, 97
Mediaevil	94
Mini Max	101
Mr. Roberts & the Rhodesmen	61
Oklahoma Sunshine Band	34, 96
Open Mind	72
Pat McJimsey	29, 64
Patch	33, 74
Polite Force	39, 94
Public Secret/Boulder	79
Puddin' Head	86
Raggs	88
Real People/New Elements/Akteelew/Cartunes	80
Redneck	77
Redshirt	102
Relayer	107
Rodney & the Blazers	65
Rudy Love	26, 66
Sahara	95
Sawdust Charley	36, 90
Seagull	85
Shine	82
Sideways	93
Sinners Repent/Smokey Bear	67
Sir Cuss	98
Sitting Ducks	108
Slip	99
Soldier	87
Spare Change	81
Standard American	79
Starr	92
Storm	99
Straightjack	108
Streetmasse	69
Sundance	85
Sunset	94
Sweetwater Band	98
The Benders	108
The Bishops	68
The Breakers	58
The Brotherhood	72
The Cambridge Experiment	70
The Camelots	65
The Clocks	39, 104
The Continentals	75
The Crayons	104
The Debonaires/the Keys	49
The Del Reys	107
The Dive Kings	40, 100
The Downbeats	53
The Echoes	50
The Embarrassment	37, 100
The Esquires	58
The Fabulous Apostles	57
The Fabulous Shi(r)theads	42, 106
The FunTones	105
The Group	54
The Illusions	60
The Imperials	50
The Innkeepers	87
The Jags	51
The Jerry Hahn Brotherhood	75
The Jokers	60
The Kozmen	103
The Lion's Mane	29, 56
The Livin' End	73
The Lost Souls	71
The Moanin' Glories	28, 56
The New Destination	80
The Omens	59
The Outcasts	22, 54
The Pendulums	52
The Premiers	19, 47
The Prophets	21, 62
The Ravens	48
The Rhythm Rousers	47
The Ricochets	77
The Rock-N-Tones	46
The Restless Knights	64
The Serfs	18, 52
The Smart Bros	53
The Soule Survivors	70
The Squires	50
The Tone Twisters	48
The Twisters	63
The Weasels	57
The Wileys	15, 46
Thesis	92
Tiny Lyman & the Jukes	48
Tobacco Jones	100
Tradewinds/Gold Plush Blues	67
Traveller	93
Tumbleweed/Windfall	93
Velvet Rainbow/Boogie	69
Walter Ego	106
White River	78

Courtesy of the Wichita-Sedgwick County Historical Museum

Chapter 1
A New Generation

Wichita in the 1950s loved its live music. It was a regular stop on the traveling circuits for musicians from Benny Goodman to B.B. King. Concert halls like the Forum and theaters like the Orpheum and the Miller hosted citywide events and big shows. Wichita was a "routing gig" due to its geographic location. Playing in Wichita brought in money. Sitting in a hotel room just passing through between Kansas City, Oklahoma City, and Denver did not.

There was not really a "Wichita" sound the way there was in Kansas City. There were notable musicians, however, such as Gage Brewer. Brewer ran the Shadowlands Club on north

Shadowland, courtesy of the Wichita-Sedgwick County Historical Museum

Hillside. The Shadowlands became later The Mambo Club, then a variety of clubs such as The Red Dog Saloon, The Earlybird Cafe, and then The Jail Saloon. It was as bandleader that Brewer learned of a new type of instrument, a guitar that was electrified. Brewer debuted this instrument at his club in October 1932, one of the first public performances of this instrument that eventually transformed global popular culture.

Postwar prosperity and Cold War anxiety brought with it well-paying jobs at Boeing, Beechcraft, Cessna, Coleman, and other manufacturing plants. The GI Bill helped returning veterans purchase homes and finance educations. The young men and women who went to the nightclubs during the war now had families to raise as well as disposable income to enjoy parties at the Blue Moon, or supper and dance clubs like the Candle Club. Wichita was a big enough market to bring in big name entertainment including Elvis. A young musician by the name of Johnny Cash came to Wichita on a snowy winter night to play at the Forum, and later returned for the opening of a new shopping center called Parklane Plaza.

Entertainment options also included television and radio. Stations such as KTVH and KAKE ran nationally syndicated variety shows, but also produced their own content as well, including televised music acts. Televised acts included groups such as the Bar 16 Ranch on Saturday afternoon with Bob Wiley on steel guitar and Jerry Hahn on guitar. Tom "Rock" Green, was another pioneer, along with Ed Macy. Together, Wiley, Hahn, Green, Macy, and others became the inspiration and mentors for a generation of musicians who followed.

Wichitans supported a number of clubs from the Rock Castle to the T-Bone, the Pla-Mor and the Esquire Club. A favorite venue was the Blue Moon on south Oliver across from the old Wichita airport, which opened in June 1940. Kansas was still officially dry, although local authorities were generally permissive of alcohol at these clubs so long as it was not sold openly. They flourished in the early postwar years, catering to a World War II generation, who were as much of a raucous youth culture as the baby boomers who came of age a generation later. By the late 1950s, however, the World War II generation was settling down and the party scene that electrified Wichita in the years after the war started to quiet down. Music and entertainment were changing. The big band era that dominated the 1940s was fading. The Blue Moon burned in 1960, never to be rebuilt.

The Forum, courtesy of the Wichita-Sedgwick County Historical Museum

Another hot spot, the Trig, became a Moose Lodge. A few years later, the venerable Forum was demolished to make way for a new civic center and concert hall called Century II.

By now, the young adults who returned from the war and working in the defense plants, had married and had children. By the 1950s, the first wave of those children were reaching their teenage years, prompting the community to create a new wave of junior high and high schools. As families moved to the suburbs on the edge of town, the local board of education realized that the city needed more than just the two existing high schools of North and East. The first new high school, West High, opened in 1953, serving families who lived west of the Arkansas River. Most of the city's growth, however, was to the south and east, towards Boeing and the aircraft plants. With Boeing,

> *"Leave him alone. He's having a good time. At least he's learning something!"*
> – Curtis Payne
> quoting his mother

Beechcraft, and Cessna offering decent wages, workers could afford to buy homes ranging from old wartime housing neighborhoods of Planeview and Hilltop Manor to the modest ranch houses along George Washington Boulevard to new suburban developments such as Bonnie Brae. As the children grew up to became teenagers among these ranch houses and cul-de-sacs, the need for a new high school was evident. The result was Southeast High School, which opened in 1957.

In some cases, the music programs at these high schools nurtured the first generation of rock musicians, even if unintentionally. Students who began playing in school bands went on to explore other musical forms. Outside of school, teenagers took the music training and used it to play rock & roll. At first, they were just groups of friends who played. As these bands came together, they moved to garages and backyards, playing for friends and at local parties. Those that were good enough started to get gigs and play more professional events.

Music stores provided lessons and equipment. One was that of Milo Wiley, whose son, Bob, had become a music figure in his own right, appearing on television. Jerry Hahn learned to play guitar at the Wiley shop and showed such promise that he started appearing on television with Bob Wiley as a teenager. The Wiley store was one of the main sources of guitars and amplifiers. It was one of the first stores to offer, in the late 1940s, the Fender

Wiley Music Company; courtesy of Carol Wiley

electric guitar. Another guitar teacher was Chuck Dooling, who ran Paramount Music. Still another was that of Jim Starkey, who in 1954 started operating the Jim Starkey Music Center in Riverside. Like Wiley, Starkey, was a television personality, appearing on Channel 10's "IGA Party Line."

The electric guitar was central. Harry Dobbin started playing guitar at age 10 on a Harmony Broadway that was given to him by his aunt. He began learning and playing songs by Peter Paul & Mary and Bob Dylan. Dobbin got his first electric guitar, a Conrad, a cheap Japanese-made Stratocaster copy bought by his father.

He wanted to play Louie Louie and having an electric guitar was crucial. That Conrad paired with a Gretsch amp was his first real "rig." Dobbin soon traded his Conrad plus $140 for a 50s gold top Les Paul. The Gretsch amp was later traded in for a blonde Fender Bandmas-

Chuck Dooling courtesy of Doug Webb

ter. However, other instruments had their own fans. No band was complete early on without a saxophone and keyboards and amplifiers were essential as well. Bands had to search for drummers and those who had amplifiers.

The story of the Bonner Brothers, Fred (East High class of '57) and John (Southeast High, class of '63) tells a story of not just the impact of early rock & roll in Wichita, but indicates the impact these early years had on kids all across America. Fred was a pioneer of sorts. A member of this first wave of distinctly American rock & roll, Fred got his start by playing drums in his parent's basement in the 1950s after discovering a drum kit under the tree for Christmas. He went on to play with bands like Dennis Hunt and the Hunters, with whom he recorded a self-produced 45 rpm local hit "Story Untold." The band later even opened for Eddie Cochran. Dennis Hunt was a pioneer himself in that he was playing "black music" on the radio in an era when it had not crossed over yet. Hunt operated KSIR, which was only licensed to broadcast during the daylight hours. That obviously was a challenge in the winter time, so the summer was even more special because he could play longer in those months.

Fred's success made an impact on his younger

Teen Club Flyer, Courtesy Curtis Payne

brother. John Bonner recalls the first time he heard his older brother playing on the radio (while he was making out with a girl). That, along with watching live rock & roll in his own basement inspired him to follow in his brother's footsteps and he took up guitar.

John also attended Fred's record-listening parties. When Fred and his bandmates got their hands on a new rock & roll record, they met in the basement to listen. Using the turntable to slow the music they worked out their individual parts. Fred had connections to the local radio stations, through Dennis Hunt which enabled him to get access to records before they received airplay. Hunt had access to more than just records; he had a deal with the tuxedo rental shop Randall's where he outfitted the band with matching tuxedos in everything from powder blue to red.

During a junior high talent show, John's band performed live rock & roll to an ecstatic crowd. While the response was positive, it was not received nearly as well by the administrators. When told to stop playing, John's band kept going to the crowd's delight. When the curtains were closed, they kept playing, only stopping when the administrators simply killed the power to the band's amplifiers.

In the 1950s and 1960s, live bands provided the entertainment, so there was no shortage of venues. The high school scene was a constant stream of events, from homecomings to proms. There was the "TARP" (Teen Age Recreation Program) at the community centers in Planeview and Hilltop. The National Guard Armory hosted dances and events. The east and west sides of town, always rivals, had their own venues for these dance parties, which would often be attended by hundreds of kids. Teen parties took place across town in places like the Hanger, the East high School gymnasium, while the west side kids took the name and spelled it backwards for their own club--Regnah. Social outlets were not as abundant, especially for kids, and church dances offered sock hops with doo-wop and other secular music as a way to provide young people a safe and socially acceptable place to gather. Dawson Methodist, the basement of Mayflower Congregational Church, and the social hall of Plymouth Congregational Church were the scenes of regular dances, The Catholic Youth Association hosted gatherings as well.

At a time when there were only three television stations, the local networks got involved in holding some of the local teen dance parties. Kids could watch from home, or they could get their parents to drop them off, where they could dance to records being played along with occasional local rock & roll bands, who got to do a few songs. Bass player and singer Bucky Walters regularly played on The KAKE TV Dance Party which aired on Saturday afternoons, and would often broadcast from surrounding, smaller towns. These programs hosted awards for best dressed girl and boy and had daily, monthly and yearly dance

Hi Fi Hop; courtesy of KWCH-TV

contests. Tom Leahy had been a disc jockey on KAKE Radio, and later hosted a show called "Irwin's Dance Party" on KAKE TV. KTVH, now KWCH, had Hi-Fi Hop, that aired daily after school, Monday through Friday from 4:30 p.m. to 5:30 p.m., hosted by Bill Brooks. Big events might take place at teen dances at the newly-opened Cotillion or at the Kiddieland Amusement Park, both of which also hosted Sunday afternoon events.

The early 1950s was still a time of segregation, when whites and blacks lived in separate worlds, each with their own music. Wichita occasionally hosted black musicians as well as whites. Chuck Berry played to a mixed audience at Joyland. B.B. King played at the Mambo Club, a black nightclub located in the old aircraft hangar where Gage Brewer once operated the Shadowlands.

A few white kids like longtime Wichita entertainer/musician Bucky Walters who had black friends and came to listen. Walters liked what he heard.

There were also times when a club had black musicians for a white audience and during breaks the band had to go outside rather than relax in the clubs themselves. The African American club scene tended to be concentrated along 9th Street east of Cleveland, with venues like the Cotton Club being well known. Nearby, places like the Zanzibar Club, Smart's Palace and the Hillside Club helped support a generation of black artists.

It seemed like a scene out of American Graffiti with kids, cars, main street, girls and fights, especially after football games when cars passed each other with horns blaring. Music blasted from the car radios. A rite of passage, at least for middle class white kids, was "Dragging Douglas," cruising up and down Douglas Avenue, in their cars, radio cranked, hanging out with friends. Sandy's restaurant on Grove was the turnaround on the east side and the Continental on the west side. The local music scene seemed to fit right in.

Sandys; courtesy of Curtis Payne

This early rock scene nurtured the first generation of musicians, from the Bonners to Jerry Wood. Gifted with a voice that was one minute angelic and the next soulful, Wood fronted the Peggs from the late 1950s through the mid-60s. Known for his ability to play virtually any instrument, the solid backing of the Peggs, a group consisting of Joe Martinez, guitarist, Ed Curiel on drums, and bassist Galen Sickler provided Wood a solid platform to freely solo on guitar, keyboards, sax and harmonica. The band was a regular headliner at Dearmore's Lounge and was in constant demand around the Midwest. It was also a favorite at the weekly Kiddieland outdoor pavilion dances. The group once backed up blues legend Jimmy Reed at Meadowlake. Wood's musical taste was more mature and eclectic than the average teen pop band that was being peddled on the pop charts, and when up-and-coming guitarist Clif Major inquired as to what this great music was called, Wood replied simply, "the blues."

Another of the legendary performers to rise out of the Kansas music scene, Mike Finnigan began his musical career rather inauspiciously when he formed a band to help supplement his full basketball scholarship at the University of Kansas. Along with fraternity brother Bob Snyder on bass and Tom Salisbury on guitar, and Finnigan on keys, the Serfs were born. What started as a lark, soon became more

serious. Finnigan chose a house band gig at Dearmore's in Wichita over a construction job in Kansas City arranged by KU's athletic department. By summer's end Finnigan had chosen music over academia and athletics, and the band made Wichita its new home. While some of the band members decided to return to college, Finnigan soldiered ahead with the addition of drummer Kenny "Bee" Bloomquist and tenor sax player Freddy Smith, both of whom had previously played with Bobby "Blue" Bland and James Brown.

The next few years saw the Serfs lineup change frequently and included Burt Timms on bass, guitarist Ed Macy, Mark Underwood on trumpet, and Carlton McWilliams on bass. At one point, Finnigan became a much renowned triple threat when he sang, played keys, and took over bass duties by playing the bass lines on the Hammond B-3 foot pedals. When the Serfs warmed up for Wilson Pickett at The Cotillion, Pickett hired Carlton "Frog" McWilliams on the spot. Carlton went on to play with Picket for years and then later with Fats Domino. Unlike other regional bands that were churning out the British beat or a Motown review, the Serfs-- with the addition of Larry Faucette on congas, Rich Margolis on vibes, and Lane Tiegen taking on guitar and songwriting duties-- rested somewhere between rhythm and blues and a somewhat Latin influence.

Nor were the Serfs simply a live act. The band recorded a single, "Bread and Water," in 1966 and while playing in New York City in 1968, the band was signed by Capitol records and recorded an album entitled, *The Early Bird Café*. While recording the album, Finnigan, Smith and Faucette were asked to play on two Jimi Hendrix songs for *Electric Ladyland*. After the album was released the band returned to Wichita and opened up a club using the Serf's album title as its name. Soon after, the band broke up-- with members going their own ways. Finnigan continued his musical career and has logged studio time and road gigs with many of the biggest names in the music industry.

In addition to the bands were the promoters. In the late 1950s, for example, Bucky Walters and the Premiers had been doing work for a local station that arranged for them to perform at Joyland with Chuck Berry, followed two weeks later by a similar arrangement at Joyland for Jerry Lee Lewis. When Lewis did not show up, the promoters of the event made the best they could of the situation. They brought in Floyd Robinson from Nashville so the event became Floyd Robinson and the Premiers. It saved the event and agent T.B. Scarning was so glad the Premieres were there that he arranged to have them tour with the Johnny Cash Show in 1959.

Among the best known local songwriters were Donnie and Diane Huffman, who grew up in Arkansas City, Kansas, developing a singing career in part with their mother's encouragement. Donnie began recording rock & roll songs, including "Pink Cadillac and a Red Headed Girl," making a few charts in the U.S. These efforts got the attention of songwriters Bill and Dorree Post, who had Donnie and Diane sing for the song "Hotrod Weekend." Donnie recalled that, "it was the summer of 1964. I'd just graduated from Southwestern College in Winfield. I was 21 and Diane was 17. "Weekend" reached No. 6 that summer." After winning KFDI'S talent contest, Donnie and Dianne recorded "Little Bitty Mini Skirt." That song reached, #11 on KFDI's charts. They also opened for The Dave Clark Five on their American Tour at the old Forum. Donnie and Diane released an album in 1972. After that, the two had shifted more to the country genre. Eventually, Donnie toured with his in-laws, the Connors. He remembered that "we ran in to Earth Wind and Fire in Ohio during the Ohio State Fair as well as the Osmonds, Pat Boone and family, Merle Haggard, and Bob Hope. (They were) all staying at the hotel where we were playing. (We) met them, hung out with them which resulted in some great stories. (We) also met Tom Jones in Philadelphia while we were performing at the Hilton at Valley Forge."

In these early days, the boundaries between rock & roll, country, rhythm & blues, and other music was a lot more fluid, as the early careers of Johnny Cash and Elvis attested. Locally, this was the golden age of the "horn band," with no group complete without a saxophone, if not also a Hammond B-3 organ or even accordion. Bands like the Rock-N-Tones, Premieres, Tiny Lymon and the Jukes, The Rhythm Rousers, and the Jags were known for their stylish tuxedos and soaring pompadours. It was a world that, in the middle 1960s found itself overwhelmed by an entirely different style of rock music coming to America from across the ocean.

The Jags

Formerly Shadowland, the Mambo Club, the Early Bird Cafe, The Jail and The Red Dog Saloon

Formerly The Lancers East and The White House

Chapter 2:
The British Invade the Midwest

In the early 1960s, rock music was a mixture of blues-influenced figures, the folk music scene of Bob Dylan, soul music, and the surf genre. Wichita's music scene looked to all areas, Wichita's landlocked position became an ironic selling point in the surf classic movie Endless Summer, which debuted in Wichita in 1966. The rationale was that if it could play in Wichita, it could play anywhere. This was the time when groups like The Breakers were at their height of popularity.

> *"Corvettes. Girls... all came with being in a band in the '60s."*
> – Fred Bonner

The Wichita rock music scene changed forever on February 9, 1964, as did the music across the nation. That evening, The Beatles appeared on the Ed Sullivan show, exposing youth to a whole new expression of rock music. It took the British Invasion to bring blues back to America, and in essence, cheated a lot of originators out of credit.

As the decade unfolded, rock music transitioned from sock hops to become the voice of rebellion and social change. Popular culture was changing with new music, new looks, and even new slang. It took some time for the change to set in. There are stories of bands finishing a set and not realizing they received a compliment when told, "you cats are bad!" The electric guitar was an important instrument in the 1950s, as Elvis and Buddy Holly showed, but nothing like what it would be in the 1960s. After the Beatles, the electric guitar was king. Bob Dylan's switch from acoustic to electric guitar was part of a larger movement. Some musicians half joked that when the Beatles came on the scene, thousands of saxophone players lost their jobs. It was an overstatement but it makes a point: the days of the horn band were numbered.

Even the structure of the band was shifting. In the 1950s, the lead singer was the key member of the group. Groups tended to be the standard "name of the lead singer and the…" Now the band, as a whole, was the key. The Outcasts were among a new group of bands that included the Illusions, Albatross, the Prophets, and the Fabulous Apostles.

The Prophets were another group formed in mid-1960s on the heels of the British Invasion, a quartet comprised of Phil Black and Dave Rice on guitars, Doug Trowbridge on bass and Jim "Mouse" Beggs on drums. They focused on tight harmonies and a repertoire that ran the gamut from the Mersey Beat to Motown. Later, the band's members included, along with Black, singer Mike Daniels, Danny Persone on drums, and Jim Kent on keyboards. The band was a local favorite performing at teen clubs such as Howard's, the Attic, and the Carrousel as well as sock hops and high school dances around Kansas. With the addition of Dell Cady on bass, the band opened for the Beach Boys at the Wichita Forum. When Phil Black approached the microphone and said "Hello Wichita," in a mock-English accent, pandemonium broke loose. When observed peering through a crack in the stage door following their performance, the band was

The Prophets, Courtesy of Phil Black

besieged by adoring fans and forced to seek refuge backstage until the crowd dispersed.

The Beatles were more than just performers. They also wrote their own songs. Rather than adapt traditional blues songs and melodies, the British Invasion unveiled a regular stream of new songs. At first, songs related to the typical teenage topics of love and romance. As the decade wore on, the Beatles and their peers became more experimental, writing songs that ranged from psychedelic to protest anthems.

The Beatles, along with the Who, the Rolling Stones, and others, became the benchmark that many of these teen bands strove for. The band as a whole was the focus. The Hammond organ using the Leslie speaker cabinet was becoming an important part of rock music. The organ could cover the horn parts of a band. The Beatles, however, had made the guitar king and scores of young musicians flooded to music stores to get their guitars. It also made guitarists very common and a number of bands rotated out guitarists and vocalists on a regular basis. Drummers and keyboardists, however, were a lot less common. In a number of cases, when bands broke up and formed new groups, the drummer was part of the nucleus of the next venture.

Young musicians still admired guitarist Tom "Rock" Green, who played with the Squires. Another important player was Clif Major, who began his career playing in garage bands in the late 1950s. Major was one of the early Wichita "gunslingers," According to Ron Starkel, bassist for the Illusions, Clif was "scary good." Major's band, the Outcasts, was formed in 1965 and was one of Wichita's early successful teen acts. They played early Yardbirds and Rolling Stones covers. The band bore proudly Jim Kent's moniker of their perceived social standing. The original Outcasts included Clif Major on guitar, Mike Daniels on vocals, Jim Kent on keys and vocals, Bruce Underwood on drums, and Johnny Bills on bass. Many musicians, however, were more familiar with the band's second lineup that included Darryl Osborn as the singer, Wayne Avery and Clif Major on guitars, Doug Emrick on bass, and Neal McGaugh on drums. Playing in various local battle of the bands competitions, the Outcasts played alongside the Illusions, Weasels, and Mother Goose.

Looking back on how rock changed during his career, John Stewart of the band Tumbleweed mused that the music went through a series of stages. At first, it was popular dance music and what mattered was how it inspired audiences to get up onto the dance floor. That had been the hallmark of the horn bands of the late 1950s and 1960s. As the 1960s, unfolded, Stewart found that local musicians such as Mike Finnigan and Jerry Wood, among others,

strove to distinguish themselves through their skill in handling difficult pieces. Most local bands did not write their own music, so a point of pride was how close one replicated an original piece by one of the era's most famous rock bands, especially when those pieces allowed them to show off their technical mastery.

On the other hand, the ability to improvise was highly valued. Perhaps the best-known example was when the Yardbirds played at the Cotillion. When the Yardbirds' drummer could not play, Neal McGaugh happened to

The Outcasts, Courtesy Marty Osborn

be in the audience. The Outcasts did Yardbirds material and McGaugh got to be the substitute drummer for the show. Later, after the Yardbirds had split-up and a new band featuring Jimmy Page was being formed, McGaugh's mother got a call from someone in a new band that would be known as Led Zeppelin. McGaugh did not get the message until much later, so the story goes.

The music continued to change. Early in his music career, Harry Dobbin was playing songs by the Kingsmen, Beach Boys, Buddy Holly and Motown artists before the Beatles came along. After the Beatles, Dobbin formed Harry & The Bushmen in 1965 and played their first gig on his 16th birthday in 1966 at the Annex, a 3.2 bar where legally, he was not allowed access. By the late 1960s, the Bushmen, perhaps the first Wichita rock & roll band to have a light show, played in places like Frontier City, West Wichita's large skate rink.

Not all rock musicians liked the change. When asked what they thought of the Beatles, one musician affiliated with the Rock-N-Tones was clear about what that group first thought about the Beatles: "we thought they sucked." The Rock-N-Tones had come from the horn band era, where crisp, tight music and clear singing was the ideal. The Beatles played what to them sounded rough, untuned, garbled music. Besides, they did not have a saxophone player and everyone knew that one could not have a real rock band without a saxophone!

The British Invasion also influenced what was being sold at music stores. One of the best known music stores was Phil Uhlik's. Uhlik Music on west Douglas had been a Wichita fixture. At one time having four locations, Uhlik started in the late 1950s in El Dorado but found his way to Wichita by the 1960s. Phil notes that his willingness to "wheel and deal," whether by installments or trading helped his customer base by putting instruments in their hands. Uhlik did more than provide equipment. Uhlik credits hiring local musician Duane Zambo for helping get a location on Waterman, known as The Workshop, that gave bands a place to play and hang out.

Phil Uhlik, radio station KLEO, and Richard Leslie helped sponsor the Battle of the Bands that took place at the Cotillion. Located on west Kellogg, the Cotillion, or the "round mound of sound" as coined by longtime Wichita DJ Phil Thompson, was a popular place for local music. Its iconic band shell was a holdover from big band-era performance venues and was a way of projecting the sound out in those years before modern amplification systems. Richard Leslie, who worked as a janitor at the Cotillion and played guitar in his band, The Bird & the Worm, suggested that the Cotillion's success could be attributed to its variety, featuring bands both,"…on the way up and on the way down." Shows ranged from national level acts like the Yardbirds to "pillow concerts," where the crowd actually sat on pillows, to Mexican and African-American bands to country-rock concerts held in connection with KFDI.

For rock fans of the 1960s, the Cotillion was famous for its rock battles. Battles drew 400 to 500 people at a cost of a dollar per ticket. Judging was informal: the fans placed their tickets in the ballot box with their favorite band's name. To the audience, it was a social event. For the bands, however, it was a time to compete and play for a large crowd. The winners won credit towards much needed music gear and got notoriety that could gain more work. Local companies like RC Cola took note of who the strong bands were and offered them contracts to write local commercial jingles. Some of the best of the bands were the Outcasts, the Jokers, the Moanin' Glories, and the Soul Survivors. The horn bands like the Breakers and the Fabulous Apostles were also battling for their share.

The Cotillion; courtesy of WSU Special Collections

There were so many events geared to young people that from the late 1960s through the mid-1970s, the Wichita Beacon geared a separate section of the paper to young adult readers. Coming out each Wednesday on peach colored paper, the section highlighted news and issues such as school functions, fashion trends, major events, social and political commentary, and car culture. Music discussions also took place, including a "Disc-Ussion" of music trends from KEYN's J. Robert Dark and record reviews by Little John Frederickson. When major groups came to town, the "peach section" of the paper covered it. There were also occasional profiles of local musicians such as Mike Finnigan, the Jerry Hahn Brotherhood, and the Moanin' Glories. By the 1970s, it hosted polls of popular national and local groups. In addition, the section had a large classified section where equipment could be bought and sold, bands could advertise for members, or offer themselves for hire. For a decade, the peach section was an essential part of life for young Wichitans.

The section's commentary also illustrated how rapidly Wichita's music tastes were shifting, keeping up with national trends. When a major rconcert at Century II in 1970 brought in big names like Chuck Berry, The Shirelles, Bill Halley and the Comets, and Bo Diddley, the section ran a series of bemused articles about how amazing it was that Wichita kids still flocked to what had become "old style" rock concerts. A related article lamented that Wichita youth wanted more current shows and argued that "teens don't want teenybopper groups" anymore.

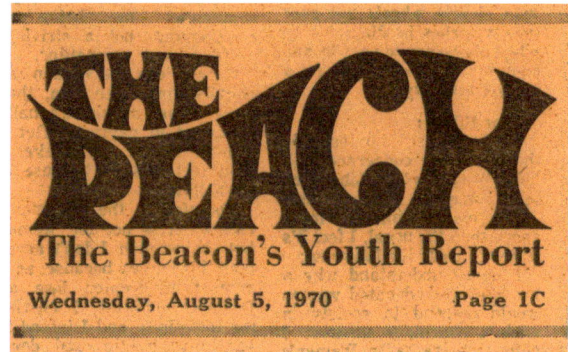

Courtesy the Wichita Beacon

Although rock music was the very symbol of youthful rebellion in the 1960s, that rebellion was sometimes more image than reality. Parents were the ones who bought the guitars and amplifiers, as when Art Martinez, who played with Doug and the Inn-truders, recalled the joy of his mother going down to Jenkins music store to buy him his bright red electric guitar with gold pegs. Parents patiently allowed their kids to take over basements, sewing rooms, and garages to practice and play, as in the case of Mike Lamb and David Gregory, who operated their own mini-radio station, KOOL at 1300 am, out of their bedroom as a part of their regional science fair project.

Jenkins Music; courtesy of WSU Special Collections

Many of these budding musicians started in their middle teens and were too young to drive. They relied on parents as well as friends to take them to gigs, at least until they were old enough to drive themselves. Parents were also the ones who had to drive 14-and 15-year-old musicians to gigs. A number of old band members, when asked about what their parents thought, recalled that their folks may not always have liked the new music, but were not opposed to their children playing it. Guitarist and singer Curtis Payne recalled his father being upset that he wasn't playing country music, but his mother chimed in to let him go ahead saying, "He is having a good time. At least he's learning something." Learning to play a musical instrument was seen as a good thing, even if the folks were a little concerned about whether the Beatles constituted good music.

Some parents even helped their kids host events. On weekends, when adult clubs had little business, they would rent out space to other groups, including youth events. Curtis Payne recalled that his dad arranged to lease the Bunny Club, a local strip club, to open up for teenagers on Sunday afternoons. Bands played at the "Teen Bunny Club" surrounded by cages that go-go dancers used at night.

A number of bands had parents as managers. The managers of the Mad Hatters were the parents of bassist Jay Bruff. Bruff's father was a police officer and his mother also worked for the police force, so it would have been hard for the group to get too rowdy. For Doug and the Inn-Truders, it was Doug Terbush's mother, Millie, who really pushed the young musicians to get out and play more. Linda Saffier, who toured with the Moanin' Glories, recalled that arriving at a new gig out of town inevitably involved a collect call to the parents to let them know everyone made it safe.

The year that saw the Beatles come to the U.S. also saw the Gulf of Tonkin incident bringing the U.S. deeper into the conflict in Vietnam. In the years that followed, the draft took its toll on the local music scene as kids, especially from blue collar families, started to go overseas. Bassist Phil Snow recalled the draft really "busted up bands." Many of the first wave of musicians such as John Bonner, Phil Black, and Jim Kent went into the military, even going into

Courtesy: Jim Kent

boot camp together. Bonner went to Vietnam, returning in 1966 and picking back up where he left off in Wichita's music scene. Jim Kent went over but still wanted his Harmony guitar. The guitar was shipped to him and made it to "Nam" without incident. Then, soon after, a firefight ensued and in the process, Kent's beloved guitar took several rounds. Other musicians were not so lucky. Singer Mike Daniels was killed in September of 1967 in Vietnam. As the conflict continued, several bands broke up as various members went to serve in the armed forces, among them, for example was The Brotherhood, a band made up of students from East High.

Not everybody chose to go serve in the military and some took their inspiration from Woodstock and other events when rock music was part of the anti-war movement. Some recalled how during World War II, their parents picked up rifles and went to war to change things whereas they picked up musical instruments.

Turning 18 also involved attending college for many. While some attended Wichita State University, others went to the more inexpensive Butler County Community College in El Dorado, Kansas, creating its own vibrant scene there that attracted some of Wichita's musicians like Clif Major and Jim Meyer. Ron Starkel, a member of the El Dorado band, the Illusions, remembers The Cage as a prime spot to play. The Cage was a teen hot spot in those days in El Dorado, a huge venue in a town with not many other options. Another band from El Dorado, The Weasels, even transitioned into writing and playing their own material. The Weasels frequently played Wichita venues including Hi-Fi Hop on Channel 12. Members of The Weasels and The Illusions became friends with Major and The Outcasts, furthering the connection between Wichita and El Dorado musicians. The Outcasts and Lion's Mane, both from Wichita played at the Cage which paid as much as $250 per night. This even attracted the Blue Things, a well known touring band out of Lawrence, Kansas.

College and universities, clubs, and bands also tied into the emerging counterculture that was

making its presence felt in Wichita. The city's ties to the Beat Movement ran deep, back to the 1950s, when several local artists and writers went to San Francisco. Wichita's ties to the Beats were so strong that when Beat icon Allen Ginsberg toured the country while on a Guggenheim grant in 1966, he made sure to visit Wichita and experience the city that shaped so many of his friends in San Francisco. While here he read poetry at the Magic Theater Vortex, with the Outcasts providing the music. Not everyone was enthusiastic about Ginsberg's presence. Conservative local leaders

Photo courtesy: Chloie Airoldi-Watters

were nervous and the police were instructed to arrest the poet immediately if things "got out of hand." It was at the student union ballroom at Wichita State University where Ginsberg first read Wichita Vortex Sutra, his powerful anti-Vietnam poem that contrasted the placidness of the Kansas landscape with the horrors of the war in Southeast Asia.

In the 1960s the music scene and the counterculture scene continued to unfold especially around Wichita State University. South of campus, near 17th and Fairmount, was a small business district where the city's first head shop, Wichita Toad and Tire was located. A few years later, the space was occupied by Jack's Green Dragon Bookstore, a beloved used book business. A popular sandwich shop, The Grinderman, was also located at the south end of the building. Nearby on 21st street stood A Blackout, a bar that featured occasional acts such as Patrick O'Connor, Bill Garrison, and Harry Weldon. Along Hillside was the Penthouse, a bar and music venue that catered to the university crowd, It was at the Penthouse where musicians like Danny Loveland and his band Blue Banana became a well-known house band.

The campus itself offered opportunities for both local and national musicians to play--or almost play in certain cases. The best known near concert was that of Jimi Hendrix. Hendrix played in Wichita as the opening act for the Monkees and was emerging on the national scene following the Monterey Pop Festival, Hendrix was scheduled to play Wichita State's Cessna Stadium in early 1969, but cancelled due to low advance ticket sales. Hendrix and his band continued on to Boulder, Colorado. A few weeks later, Hendrix catapulted to icon status at Woodstock. A few years later, Rod Stewart, who was with the band Faces at the time actually did play at Cessna Stadium.

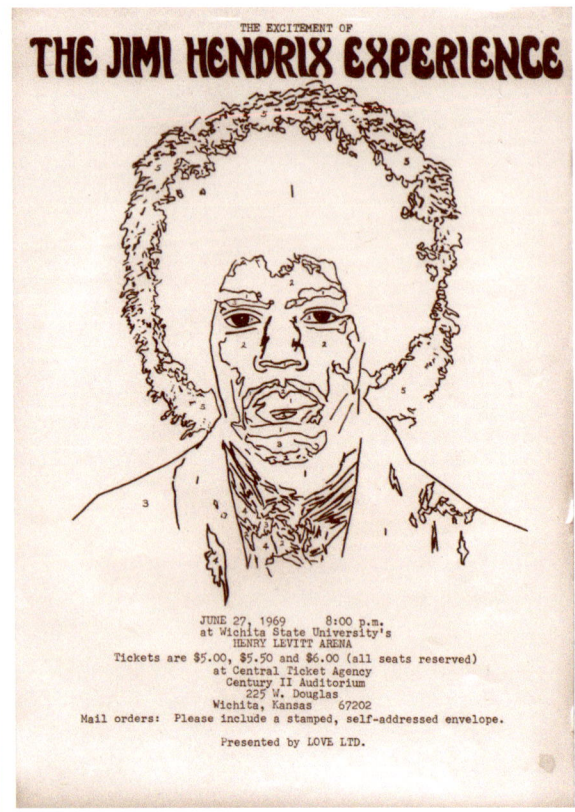

The following year, Wichita State saw a similar near concert take place when, in the wake of Woodstock, Great Plains Peace Productions and KEYN organized a "Peace Festival" at Cessna Stadium that was to have showcased Canned Heat. Canned Heat did not show up, however, but the event continued anyway.

The area was also a center of tensions over Civil Rights. For Wichita's youth, times were becoming tense as the decade unfolded. In 1967, a decision to eliminate black teenagers from the cheer team at East High resulted in a fight between white and black students at the popular Sandy's Drive In on Douglas Avenue. In August 1968, a group of white men shot two black men along 17th Street and a fight erupted between blacks and whites at the Penthouse, the start of a series of incidents that resulted in the mayor ordering all clubs, taverns, and liquor stores in the area closed temporary, with National Guardsmen patrolling the streets of northeast Wichita in tanks.

The area around Wichita State was the boundary between primarily white areas to the east and primarily black neighborhoods to the west. Paralleling the white clubs were African-American establishments such as Flagler's Garden hosting both local and traveling entertainment. A black club district along 9th street developed including The Sportsman as well as The Elks Club.

Here, young musicians like Rudy Love emerged and became popular with both white and black audiences. "My whole life has been a musical journey," Love later recalled. It was a journey that began very young and included the formation of a gospel group by the fifth-grade. As a young adult, Love went on the road with Little Richard and Ray Charles before returning to Wichita, where he formed Rudy Love and the Love Family Band. His career did not stay local, however. He was a demo vocalist for Motown Records, worked with musicians such as Marvin Gaye and groups such as Sly and the Family Stone.

Another respected African-American musician from the time was Berry Harris. Originally from Chockie, Oklahoma, Harris began playing in bands in Muskogee before coming to Wichita in 1956. He initially played at the Bomber Club near McConnell Air Force Base and later became a fixture in the black music scene. By the 1970s, Harris had become well known for his work in groups like The Jive Five. More than just a club musician, Berry was a fixture in the local blues scene, which included many of the original Wichita rock & roll musicians. Although he was well regarded in the African-American community,

Harris found that the white music fans gave him city-wide recognition.

While the community struggled with segregation, a number of musicians challenged the color barrier. White musicians could go to black clubs provided they went with friends. A few bands had mixed membership. Among the better known was Lotus, which included John Smith as vocalist.

Diversity was more than just black and white. Latino musicians were an important part of the scene right from the start. Among them was Dolphie Ybarra of the Fantabulous Jaggs, whose prominent pompadour was hard to miss! A number of early musicians were Latino like Joe Martinez and Ed Curiel of the Peggs or Art Martinez and Mike Jimenez of Doug and the Inn-Truders. Meanwhile, south-side bands had their own Latino musicians, such as Montezuma's Revenge featuring Paul Chavez on bass and Danny "Bubba" Martinez on vocals.

Individual members came from a wide range of backgrounds. The Chinese-American Mar family operated the Colony Club. The Mar's kids, Danny and Lindy, even played in the club's band, Crystal Saints. Andy Gore of the Moanin' Glories came from a locally known Jewish family. Native American Baptiste "Bat" Shunatona of the Soul Survivors had a rich lineage with the Otoe-Missouria people. Given the number of musicians whose families came from Oklahoma, it is likely that many others had Native ancestry even if they did not sport the identity the way some did.

Former site of the Penthouse club

Former site of Dearmores and Tennessee Beer Mill & Tennesse Gin Mill

Chapter 3
The Grind

By the late 1960s, the band scene started to change as 13- and 14-year old high school musicians turned 18. A big change for most bands was when some in the group were old enough to drive and have their own cars. Without having to rely on friends or parents to take them to gigs, these slightly older musicians were freer to play later and at less savory events. When they reached 18, they could drink legally, or at least beer, since hard liquor was only allowed to those 21 and older. This

> *"3.2 beer kept Rock & Roll Alive."*
> – Randy Crump

opened a whole additional set of clubs and locations. Bars near McConnell Air Force Base catered to a very different crowd than the one that went to the Teen Bunny Club. Then, there were the frat parties at the University of Wichita, later Wichita State University.

Kansas and alcohol have long had a complicated relationship. From 1881 through 1949, Kansas was officially a dry state, although enforcement of the law varied. During World War II, Wichita's nightclubs and dance clubs operated more or less openly, setting the stage for a repeal of statewide prohibition in 1949. Even then, however, determining who could offer alcohol was a challenge. From 1965 until 1987, when liquor by the drink was legalized, alcohol could only be served in clubs to "club members," often just a token cost for a membership card. Even airlines were prohibited from serving alcohol while flying over the state.

Local DJ Randy Crump noted that 3.2. beer kept rock alive in Wichita. Technically, beer that contained up to 3.2 percent alcohol was a "cereal malt beverage" and could be sold openly. This, along with the fact that the drinking age was 18, for beer at least, provided the basis for a number of clubs which served the youth market in general and older teenagers in particular. There were many 3.2 clubs, located all around town, including the Draft Board, located in a converted storefront, the Green Onion, the King Cole Inn, and the Stage Door Inn, with the dance floor made out of the salvaged wood from a local bowling alley.

It was once commonplace to know the whereabouts of a Midwestern road band as a distant DJ from Oklahoma City, Oklahoma proclaimed, "KOMA proudly presents….."

In the 1960s and 1970s, the era was dominated by several key bands. Early on, it was the Moanin' Glories and Lion's Mane. By the mid '70s it was Board of Regents and Hard Road. The Moanin' Glories included Ritchie Kunkle on guitar, Karl Berkebile on keys, Andy Gore on bass and Marc Mourning on drums. The quartet fashioned a British-flavored rhythm and blues sound that made them a staple around the Midwest. In fact, the band spent so much time on the road that an appearance in their hometown of Wichita was considered a special event.

Kunkle and Gore first met in '65 at a party while still in junior high school. With a shared interest in music, they decided to form a rock & roll band, the Candles. After working unsuccessfully with several percussionists, Marc Mourning was finally chosen as the group's drummer. Later, when a keyboard player was needed, he suggested his cousin Karl Berkebile. The band changed its name to the Moanin' Glories-- a pun on the drummer's last name as well as a nod to the '60s flower power movement. For the next six years the band worked weekends and summers on the road playing teen dances, clubs, and parties. Some groups

Courtesy: The Moanin' Glories

played only part time. The Moanin' Glories were full-time musicians, with exotic British Vox equipment that the Beatles influenced.

In the summer of '67, the group released a self-penned record entitled, "She took the Rain Out of My Mind" backed with "You Better Watch Out."

Formed in 1965, the Lion's Mane was comprised of Greg Skaff on guitar, piano and vocals, Rich Ridder on bass and vocals, and Dan Monnat on drums and vocals. The band was known for their polished arrangements

Courtesy: The Lion's Mane

and tight vocal harmonies. A typical set included songs by groups as diverse as the Beatles, Traffic, The Band, and James Brown. In 1966, the band added Tom Coleman on keys and vocals. Two years later, Coleman was replaced by Stan Spurrier. In 1969, Ridder left the group which soldiered on without the benefit of a bass player. The Lion's Mane was a local favorite and could be seen at such venues as the Attic, Meadowlake Beach, and the Odessa Club. As local music afficionado Mark Archibald recalled "The Lion's Mane was my favorite local band. I saw them every chance I could."

Another musician was Pat McJimsey, who had a voice steeped in the blues and the ability to wring plaintive notes from his guitar. McJimsey began fronting bands at 17 with Velvet Honey, a group that rehearsed in his mother's garage in southeast Wichita. By the late 1960s, McJimsey had formed the Bear Valley Blues Band, with regular appearances at Meadowlake Beach and the Nomar Theater.

McJimsey later fronted acts such as the Entire British Navy and Four Brothers. He also shared the stage, as an opening act, for a wide variety of artists such as Canned Heat and Spyro Gyra. He toured with Finnigan & Wood, Leon Russell and Freddy King. He also did stints

Courtesy: Pat McJimsey

with Patch and the KFDI Ranch House Swing Band. A natural blues artist, McJimsey was nonetheless at home with any genre of music. He performed with many different Wichita area jazz groups as featured vocalist.

Events like battles of the bands, allowed for some friendly competition, but the musicians were usually too busy to see each other perform, let alone clash.

This was a late-night business. It was not uncommon for a band to get done with a last set at nearly 2 a.m., go out for something to eat, or wind down at after-parties before going to sleep as the sun came up. Late-night diners were almost as important as clubs and music stores. They included the Nifty Kitchen, Denny's, Brownie's, and the Fairland Cafe. Some places even named some of their sandwiches after local bands.

Some bands wrote their own music, but for the most part, they played songs from the popular groups of the time. A number of local bands mirrored the sound and influence of popular national bands.

The Prophets tended to reflect the Beatles. The Outcasts tended to reflect the Rolling Stones and the Animals. Bear Valley Blues Band was similar to Canned Heat.

These bands and lineups tended to be short lived, lasting for only two to three years before either bringing in new musicians or breaking up, with the members finding new roles in new bands. When the Outcasts broke up, for example, guitarist Clif Major and drummer Neal McGaugh went on to form Blue House. Meanwhile, when New Destination broke up, drummer Bill Wullschleger and guitarist Randy Rickman initially formed a duo and then added Jerry Powell on organ and Jack Howard on bass to form Velvet Rainbow.

Sometimes a band renamed itself, either in connection with a new set of members or to freshen up its image, as when Public Secret became Boulder in 1970. Sometimes, names changed because they had to. For example, when a group of musicians from Lawrence came to Wichita, they called themselves Mud Pie. However, so many clubs mistook them for the group Mud Creek, that they renamed themselves Tumbleweed, only to rename the group again to Windfall when they learned that there was already a band called Tumbleweed. By contrast, some bands continued for several years, with a number of musicians going in and out, Hard Road, and Lotus being among the best known examples.

In a number of cases, it was a musician or handful of musicians who continued to play with one another, just forming a sequence of different groups. Ron Schauf and Joe Sauer, for example, initially came together to form Top Banana and the Rest of the Bunch in 1969, which gave way to Deep Rock, the Cambridge Experiment, Shine, and Soldier before each going on to play for a wide range of bands in the late 1970s. Another example was singer Russ "Big O" Oropresa/Armitage, who was a key figure first for Harley Zurrett, then the Cyrus Noble Whiskey Band, then Southwind, and finally, Tobacco Jones. Curt Poole was a common thread for a number of groups including Boogie, Lo & Behold, and Sunset.

The longest continually performing band in Wichita, Lotus had a story that highlights just how dynamic and fluid the music scene was at the time. The story began in May 1970 when Don Overstake was discharged from the Navy. Upon returning to Wichita, Overstake received a phone call and on the other end was John Bonner, who invited him to play with Hard Road. the band needed an organist and Overstake came with a Vox Continental organ.

Courtesy: Lotus

Hard Road was playing to packed houses at the Camelot Club, but it was just too much. Overstake resigned from Hard Road and went down the street to play at the Fireside, forming a new band initially called Crow Haven Farm. In early 1972, however, the band changed its name to Lotus, the name of a band Overstake had heard while on leave in a club in Australia. Soon, the band left the Fireside to go to the Scene 70s, performing a hard-core rock sound inspired by ZZ Top and Deep Purple.

It was as the point they decided to try touring. The agent with American Bands Management booked Lotus on a set of gigs down in Texas and throughout the South. The experience was not what the group expected. Overstake recalled that it "sucked eggs" with marginal gigs and long periods of downtime, waiting in motel rooms for the call to the next venue. A few years later, the band was tired, happy to give up touring, and returned to Wichita to play Scene 70s.

One aspect of touring did make a positive impression, however. Their first gig was in Killeen, Texas, where they played at a club where people ate and listened to the band. This was very different to the scene in Wichita, where people went out to eat and then went to a club to listen to music. Unless a band was simply there to provide background music, anything stronger evoked complaints of "Turn that music off, I am trying to eat." The idea that a place could offer both food and entertainment at the same time time was a novelty that left a lasting impression on Overstake.

In other cases, the transition from the Wichita club scene to touring brought more promising results, as in the case of Danny Loveland. In 1966, Loveland was playing at the Seneca Lounge when the owners of a newly-formed club, the Penthouse on North Hillside Avenue had just opened and needed a house band. Loveland joined the band, initially named "The Centurions," and included several former members of Renegade. Soon after, the band made a record on the Kanwic label, "Spicks and Specks" under the name "Blue Banana". The recording did well, charting in 17 States and reaching #5 on the Top 40 Charts. The following year, Loveland did another recording, this time under the name Danny Loveland and the Luv Bugs. For a short time, Loveland also operated his own club, the "Draft Board," became a local promoter of concerts,

Courtesy: Blue Banana

provided the entertainment for another local venue, the Casino, and formed a sound and lighting company called Showco.

In the early 1970s, Loveland left to form the band "Shagnasty" for the sole purpose of going to California. The members included: Dick Parsley on organ, Greg Dunn on guitar, keyboards, and drums; Dave Riggins on bass and guitar; and Loveland on drums, with all members providing vocals. They played the Yankee Clipper in Santa Barbara, Grand Hotel Disneyland, and Indian Wells Hotels in Palm Springs. They were handled by McConkey Artists in Hollywood, and later by Peggy Rogers at Dick Clark Productions.

In 1972 Shagnasty disbanded and Loveland joined Bo Donaldson and the Heywoods on Peggy Rogers recommendation. The Heywoods had the #1 national hit "Billy Don't Be A Hero" in 1974. While with the Heywoods, Loveland played New Year's Eve 1972 at Disneyland, with The Friends of Distinction, and Rick Nelson in front of over 100,000 people. In 1975, Dick Clark Productions, ask Loveland to form a new band called "Loveland," recording "Black is Black" and several other songs on the "Artist of America" Label in 1976. By 1977, however, Loveland was back in Kansas, having opened "Carats Palladium," the largest teenage Disco in Kansas.

A lot of these bands, at least early on, had goals of recording and releasing an album. Going on the road expanded a group's exposure. When a steady, weekly gig was not secured, going on the road was also a way to survive. "The grind" offered steady work but for real success, musicians from Wichita had to leave for the coasts to break into the music scene. This was the case for Mike Finnigan, Jerry Wood, Rudy Love and many others. In search of greener pastures, the Moanin' Glories moved to the east coast in 1970 and performed around the Boston area before securing an eight-week tour of Japan. By 1971, the band believed they had exhausted every avenue and disbanded.

For most bands, Wichita's bustling club scene provided lots of opportunities to play. Venues like the Seneca Lounge; the Fireside; Colony Club; Dearmore's (Later the Tennessee Gin Mill and Beer Mill); Lancers East, The White House; Camelot Club; Scene 70s; Sound Sircus; the Chesterfield Club; Caesar's Palace; The Admiral's; Coyote Club; and Penthouse all hosted house bands. "When you became a name, the gigs called you," recalled Pat Preboth, describing how there was a time when the club owners were interested in locking down their house bands. There were an array of venues, from the upscale Candle Club to the Phone Booth, a classic "Hippie Joint" with pillows instead of chairs. Some clubs had more than one house band, as when the Red Dog Inn featured both Gentleman J and the Good Times as well as Mike Finnigan.

Two of the best known were a pair of clubs at George Washington and Harry in a location that originally housed Dearmore's but later became the Tennessee Gin Mill and the Beer Mill with the Gin Mill's house band being the country rock-themed Sweetwater. Located

A Memorable

EVENING OF

DANCING

HI HO CLUB

WICHITA, KANSAS

in the same building, the Beer and Gin Mills reflected Kansas's bizarre liquor laws. Anyone 18 and older could drink beer, but not hard liquor. That was for people over 21. Therefore, the Beer Mill catered to the 18-21 crowd and the Gin Mill catered to the over 21 crowd.

Wichita's music scene was big enough to support clusters of clubs in various parts of town. One was around Wichita State and included the Flame/Flicker and the Cedars on 13th Street, the Penthouse on Hillside, and, much later, Kirby's on 17th Street. For a time, a significant area of clubs was on or near South Seneca that, over the years, included the Stardust, the Hi Ho, the Green Onion, Fun Au Go Go, the Spur Club, The Flame, the Seneca Lounge, the Sound Sircus, the Fireside West, and Scene 70s. In the 1960s and 1970s, this was the home of a bustling music scene. By 1979, all that remained was Scene 70s, operated by George "Doug" and Mary Hill, that operated in the building that once housed the Fireside West and before that, the Seneca Lounge.

Sometimes clubs changed bands and sometimes bands left for new opportunities. The Soul Survivors got their start at Dearmore's. A few years later, the band's membership had shifted and the group began playing at the Hi Ho. Two years later, the club's owner announced that he wanted to change out bands and the Soul Survivors had to find a new home. For a time that was the Fireside but eventually, the band found itself playing the newly-formed Sound Sircus. The group lasted until the club closed. Many of Wichita's best known bands shared similar stories.

There were clubs in nearby towns like El Dorado and Hutchinson and whole scenes in places like Lawrence, Manhattan, Kansas City and Denver where groups who went on tour could play. There were even stories of bands that found themselves double booked and so, the vocalist and drummer might go to one gig while the main guitarist and bassist went to another, with friends coming in to fill the other roles at the respective gigs. As a result, there were times when two bands literally played two venues at once!

While smaller bands arranged their own gigs, a number of groups operated as part of commercial agents or booking company. as when T.B. Skarning managed the gigs of the Premieres or when American Bands Management booked Lotus on its ill fated tour of the South. A Kansas-based company was Mid-Continent Entertainment, organized by John Brown and Mike Murfin, which managed groups such as the Fabulous Flippers, the Red Dogs, or the Lawrence-based Spider and the Crabs featuring the female singing component called The Rye.

It did not take long for the club scene to take its toll on musicians and club-goers alike. If a band was popular, the owner had them play every night for three months with no days off. Many bands found themselves playing five or six nights a week at the same club. Russ Oropressa/Armitage recalled how he worked third shift at Boeing, which meant he had to leave gigs before they were done just to get down to the plant to start work. It became too much for two of the band members who had regular jobs. By the 1970s, a lot of these early musicians either left for other opportunities or started to wind down and search for other, more sustainable careers. Some, like Jim Meyer, got out of performing in the early 1970s as the drug scene started and found other avenues with better opportunities. In Meyer's case, that was photography. As part of a cover band, Jim photographed the main acts after he played. Eventually, he found that photography lent itself to a career. Responsibilities like marriage and children were starting to enter the picture. John Bonner recalls this period: "There was no free time. Late nights, get home at four or five in the a.m., going to bed with the sun coming up… getting married makes it hard."

The Big Bun, courtesy of the Wichita-Sedgwick County Historical Museum

Chapter 4
Hard Rock

By the early 1970s, a new, younger group of musicians was starting to emerge. They were middle schoolers when the Beatles Invasion hit. They grew up listening to the Beatles and Rolling Stones from an early age. They were high schoolers when Woodstock happened. Their older siblings and friends played in the Battle of the Bands. It was time for them to take local rock in a new direction.

One of the members of this second wave, Pat Preboth, whose father was a Southern Baptist Minister and served at Airlane Baptist, Wichita's first Southern Baptist congregation. That position did not last, and the older Rev. Preboth went to California where the family appeared on television on an early Christian show. Pat returned to Wichita with his mother, and joined a music scene that would have horrified his father's former congregation. As a young teenager, and aspiring drummer, Pat was smuggled into clubs. He had the benefit of playing with some of the area's best musicians.

Preboth, although getting an earlier start than most was an early member of this second wave that included Jim Hill, Joe Sauer, Ron Schauf, and Kevin Brown. The first wave tended to come from schools like East and Southeast. This second wave came from a much wider variety of local high schools from across the area including Goddard, West High and Catholic schools such as Kapaun. Music teachers, or at least some of them, were moving away from the marches and swing era jazz to teach their students jazz, blues, and wider music forms. Kevin Brown, for example, found that his music teachers at West encouraged students to study jazz, but also go out and experience music, from blues and rock to church music, to get a wider background. West supported a number of bands including the Patriots and the Bue Cotts, whose members included drummer Neal McGaugh.

> "I was getting paid to have fun!"
> – Pat Preboth

Jim Hill, another of the new generation, recalled the innocent days of just a few short years earlier when he first saw Harry and Bushmen and Jay and the Mad Hatters at the Mayflower Church basement in a battle of the bands event. Then, just seeing live rock & roll was a rare thrill. By the 1970s, it was "a good night when you see a fight" in the club. Recalling one particular night outside the Mecca club after a Freddy King show, Jim recalled seeing two guys fight naked in the parking lot, a sight that did not go unnoticed by King himself, who proclaimed that having been all over the world had never seen that before. By the early 1970s, a young Jim Hill found himself performing regularly with his band Patch, initially consisting of Hill on guitar and vocals; Craig Nietfeld, bass and vocals; David Pence, drums; and Alan Baugh, Keyboards. Guitarists Chris Hutchens, Pat McJimsey, and Kent Havener played with Patch as well, as did vocalist Kenny Potter. With the slapdash fashion

Courtesy: Patch

that band was formed, the group must have figured that Patch was a perfect name. The band performed the FM album cuts that were popular in that period.

The band names and faces changed often, sometimes month-to-month. For example, in March of 1969, a group of students from Kapaun, including vocalist Joe Sauer, Brad Bartlett on drums, John Wurth on bass, Mike Wurth on rhythm guitar, and Ron Schauf on lead guitar, formed the band Top Banana and the Rest of the Bunch. Known as "the sound with appeal," they made their debut at the Mount Carmel Academy Talent Show "just for glory." They emulated musicians like Cream and the Rascals. Joe recalled playing a high school gig at Joyland saying, "the Ferris wheel would suck the power from your Leslie and B-3 organ!"

By the 1970s, rock & roll had gone from a teenage phenomenon to a major part of American culture. Record stores like Argus Tapes and Records were the place to be on new release day. Fans and musicians alike lined up on Tuesdays to get their hands on a copy of their favorite band's new album. For most young people the goal was to be on the cutting edge of music. For local musicians, the goal was to get the album as early as possible so that by the weekend their band could perform it live. Stores also sold home stereo equipment in a time where having quality hi-fi gear was essential for listening and one's status. Then, there were the music stores that sold equipment to bands as well as recording studios such as Hi Fidelity in Riverside.

The radio was just as important as the record

Courtesy: Jack Oloiver

store. Stations were locally owned and operated, years before national syndicates focused on carefully honed target markets. Each station hoped to be the first in playing a new song, regardless of whether it was a national or local release. The first major Top 40 station in Wichita was KLEO at 1480 on the dial, without competition until KEYN located at 900 on AM dial came along in 1967. KEYN-FM was followed by KFH-FM. At KFDI, a primarily country station, General Manager Mike Oatman gave his staff quite a bit of freedom to play any group or music that he thought would be popular, regardless of genre. KMUW at Wichita State University was still a student-run station at the time and played a wide range of music types and bands.

Stations in Wichita and even some from as far away as Oklahoma, like the 50,000-watt KOMA, aired the music of local bands. This gave the bands more exposure and it was a big deal to be mentioned. A band made it once it got on the air waves. Bands like the Moanin' Glories, the Fabulous Apostles, the Red Dogs, the Blue Things, King Midas & the Mufflers, etc. relied on publicity from commercials.

Courtesy: Jack Oloiver

The radio scene allowed disc jockeys to become as well-known as bands. Radio DJs became local celebrities. Mack "Kansas Mack" Sanders' KSIR was the station at 900 on the AM dial before it became KEYN. Early "underground" DJs included "Little" John Frederickson and Randy Crump who kept Wichita up to speed beyond the top 40 hits.

The psychedelic rock that was coming across these radio stations was getting heavier, louder, and longer. The first generation of rock musicians were inspired by the Beatles and the Rolling Stones. The next wave of local bands did covers of Cream, Led Zeppelin, Jimi Hendrix, the Doors, and Kansas; bands that prided themselves on technical finesse and complicated fingerings. By the 1970s, rock & roll was again in flux and became more of a performance complete with light shows and projectors.

Sometimes these events put local bands in contact with major rock musicians. Jon Weaver recalled one such encounter. Weaver had just left Traveller to play with Oklahoma Sunshine and remembered how, "one night we were playing at The Tennessee Gin Mill along with Sweetwater when a guy in pink cowboy boots, long black hair, a New York accent, and a body guard standing close, asked if he could sit in with our group. We then found out that it was Ace Frehley of KISS, who was in town to play a show. KISS always wore make up and there weren't any known pictures of them without their costumes. He favored my set up with my Goldtop Les Paul through a Marshall half stack, so I let him use my gear. Don (Neal, a guitarist with Oklahoma Sunshine) was a little intimidated and insisted that I play through his rig. We had a terrific jam playing tunes that we all knew like Johnny B. Goode, Kansas City and the like. Jeff (Pickering) made his steel sound like a fantastic slide guitar. It was an incredible night of music. "

A harder sound was gaining popularity. As

Mark Shelton recalled, "it was the 1970s and Epic Metal was not even a genre of music yet. But it was very soon that the tides and styles changed and started developing into what was going to be the standard for a whole new name for heavy, loud and evil sounding hard rock. It was the birth of Heavy Metal." This popularity inspired a group of students at North High, who formed a band called Embryo with Mark Shelton on drums and Jim Stark on guitar. Shelton then went into the Marines and upon returning, developed a band, Manilla Road, initially with Ben Munkirs on drums, Scott Park on bass and Shelton on guitar. Always edgy,

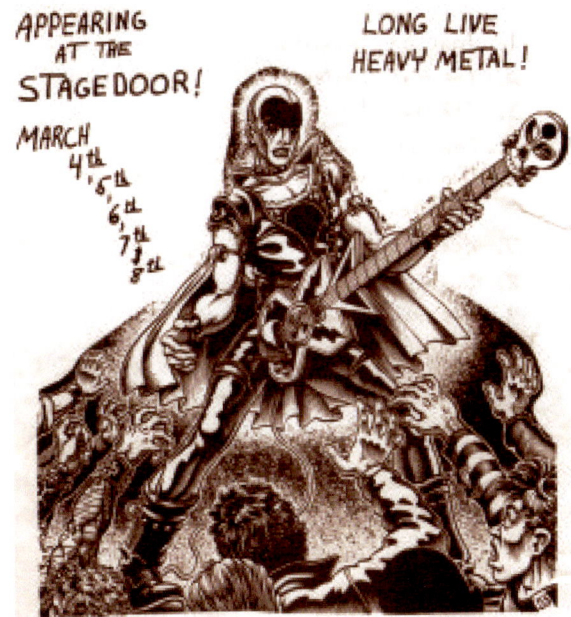

even by metal standards, Manilla Road went on to record several albums under Black Dragon Records, albums that proved to have a larger following in Europe than in the United States.

As *Rock of Ages, The Rolling Stone History of Rock n Roll* put it, the music was "turning concerts into exercises in high decibel rants and it was in the concert that the heavy metal experience was most purely obtained." Hard Rock wasn't just popular, it was profitable. Nationally, promoters and bands worked to fill huge arenas rather than just smoky night clubs. This high-volume music made sense in the large arenas but was hard to pull off for local bands. The amplifiers went from small Fender and Vox combos in the early 1960s to Marshall stacks and Kustom amps in the mid-1970s. Today, many of these musicians suffer from hearing loss because of the attempt to be louder and louder. It was also hard on the audience to be in a small club with several 100-watt amplifiers going full blast.

Music was moving out of the clubs and into the open, as seen through the number of concerts performed in the city's parks. If the battles of the bands at the Cotillion defined rock in the 1960s, summer afternoon concerts, taking place before the clubs opened, became

the mainstays of the following decade. The concerts were popular with youth but not always well received by the rest of the community, as in one instance when park officials initially prohibited the Committee for Student Rights from holding an amplified rock concert in Central Riverside Park, fearing complaints from the community. When the students complained about "selective discrimination," the park board backed down and allowed the group to hold their Sunday afternoon event.

Live rock & roll took place from Herman Hill and South Riverside Park all the way up to the grassy lawn in front of Dirksen auditorium on Wichita State's campus during the first day of classes. These were all places where big and small local bands alike played. Jim Hill remembered that his band Patch was part of "the house band of Herman Hill Park" where

bands put on free concerts every Sunday. It gave bands exposure outside of their normal club gig. However, the city was looking for a reason to shut down the concerts at Herman Hill, as they had at Riverside Park, responding to residents who did not want loud music so close to their houses.

The era of park concerts came to an abrupt end with the Herman Hill Riot that took place on Easter weekend in April 1979. Although local lore tied the event to a Ted Nugent concert

Saturday, May 17, 1969

Youths Allowed To Rock Legally With Amplifiers

The Committee for Student Rights will hold a legal musical program in Central Riverside Park Sunday using amplified sound equipment, park board officials said Friday.

An "agreement" was signed by members of the CSR and Tom Allen, recreation superintendent, to allow musical groups sponsored by CSR to use the park band shell and amplifying equipment. The agreement says the park board will furnish electricity and a public address system operator at no charge between 3 and 6 p.m. Sunday. Similar agreements are made between many groups, the park board spokesman said, citing the summer concerts held in the park.

The arrangement stems from an incident last Sunday in which members of the CSR charged "selective discrimination" when they were refused permission to use electronic amplifying equipment in a folk-rock concert on the basis noise would cause area residents to complain.

Courtesy the Wichita Eagle

that was playing at the city's Coliseum, the story began with a concert taking place at Herman Hill. Local complaints of drug use and loud noise prompted the police to arrive. The spark involved people parking their cars on the grass. When police asked that the cars be moved, tensions mounted and the crowds continued. Bassist Phil Snow remembers the incident as a boiling point between the police and the partying crowd that massed at these parks. As racial tensions increased in these years the police were equipped with new anti-riot gear and tear gassed the crowd. "They had all this stuff and no one to use it on," Snow said. The launching of tear gas incited the crowd to attack the police cars. By the time it was over, more than 50 people, both police and civilians, were injured. Over 60 people were arrested. Police from nearby areas had been called in for backup.

At the clubs, the hard, heavy music that was popular in outdoor events was so loud that other audiences started to want something more social and more danceable. Bands started to expand their line-ups to include horn sections, reflecting the change in mainstream music. Saturday Night Fever and John Travolta played a big role in pushing disco to the front. For Wichitans, the club for disco was Pogo's. Pogo's wasn't just a disco club, however, and musicians from across the spectrum played there at one time or another.

Mainstream bands and clubs had to make a choice, as Don Overstake learned as soon as he acquired the Fireside in 1975. As part of Lotus, he wanted to play a wide range of music, including songs that were creative, technical, and willing to experiment. Managing a club, however, showed that audiences generally demanded top 40, dance music, even disco. It proved hard to balance the artistic creativity of a musician with the realities of a club manager that needed a large, stable clientele.

Bands, meanwhile, had to adapt to new styles or fade away. Jim Hill recalls Patch and other bands of the era going "through an identity crisis, by 1972, Patch had become a glam rock band… then shifted to fusion, King Crimson type stuff and progressive rock…We weren't afraid to try new things." These bands had some of the most success into the 1970s for their ability to stay relevant. Bands of this time period were beginning to pick up a soundman as a regular member. Mike Metz learned the trade from being a drummer for various bands including Thesis. His expertise in electronics and sound allowed him to start working double duty, playing drums and being the sound man for some of the hottest local acts. Balloon Warfare, Sideways, the Dive Kings, and The Clocks all relied on Metz's abilities.

If there was any so called "Wichita Sound," however, it was perhaps with country rock. Where the country rock scene had an advantage was the openness to local bands performing original music. Often relegated to smaller joints on the edge of town, the country rock bands didn't always enjoy the more vibrant scene inside the city although some bands even got air time on KFDI. One was Sawdust Charley, which got its name from an old 1870s wanted poster. The band included John Dondlinger, drums; Mike Ehrke, steel guitar, guitar and vocals; Jamey Ratzlaff on guitar and vocals; Harry Dobbin on bass, guitar and vocals; and Doug Webb on guitar and vocals. They played locally at The King Cole and the Stagedoor Inn, plus a venue near Cheney called the Dry Dock Inn. They

Courtesy: Sawdust Charley

also toured across the state, made it to The Million Dollar Cowboy Bar in Wyoming, and played at the Palomino and the Troubadour in Los Angeles. Sawdust Charley considered themselves fortunate to play their original songs, eventually developing a catalog of about 60 originals. Radio stations like KFDI played a new generation of country musicians like Waylon Jennings, Jerry Jeff Walker, and Willie Nelson. A hybrid of rock music and country, "country rock," started to develop with groups like the Nitty Gritty Dirt Band. Local groups included Sawdust Charley, Potlatch, Southwind, Sundance, and Sweetwater who could owe their origin to what may have been the first country rock album, *Sweetheart of the Rodeo* by the Byrds, as well as the influence of Buffalo Springfield. Local bluegrass performers started coming together to form what became the Winfield Bluegrass Festival.

The connection between rock and country was not always easy. A lot of rock musicians dismissed country or bluegrass as the hokey music of their parents. Meanwhile, country audiences still demanded a clean-cut look on performers. While the musicians, as usual, got along just fine between themselves, crowds of country and rock fans sometimes mixed and sometimes just barely tolerated each other. Local clubs knew country rock could draw crowds but their regular patrons were not sure they liked the long-haired, scruffy crowd who showed up.

The original nature of rock & roll music was to challenge mainstream culture. By now, rock was becoming so commercial that the next generation of young musicians were about to rebel against rock itself. The era saw rise to what soon became known as punk rock with bands such as the Ramones and the Sex Pistols. Wichita was not far behind as a small contingent of musicians found one another through local advertisements to form punk rock bands. Ultimately a small number of bands evolved from the introductions that followed and these high school students moved to Wichita State University. One, in particular, performed in 1977 under the name, The Lemurs. After a short time and the departure of the singer Bart Ewonis and addition of a bass player Ron Klaus became known as The Embarrassment.

They first performed in 1979 and released a 45-rpm single in 1980, They then began traveling widely, playing well-known venues such as CBGBs and the Danceteria in New York City. After the subsequent release of several other recordings including compilations by labels

Courtesy: The Embarrassment

such as "Sub-Pop," negotiations with producer John Cale ensued. For a time, music journalists spoke of the Embarrassment in the same terms as the group REM, debating which was more relevant as up-and-comers. The group disbanded in Wichita in 1983 before commercial success was achieved. Two of its members, Bill Goffrier and Brent "Woody" Geissman moved to Boston and onto successful careers in music with Geissman joining "Del Fuegos and Goffrier starting the band Big Dipper.

As in previous decades, African-Americans faced their own challenges, including the decline of the old business district on 9th and Cleveland, and the club scene. Tensions over limited economic prospects, discrimination, and problems with police resulted in a riot along 21st Street in 1980. Orin Friesen, who served in several roles at KMUW, recalled that during the time of the race riots near Wichita State, that he sometimes spent the night at the radio station rather than risk going outside. The economics of the city itself started to change as well, with companies like Cessna, Beechcraft, Coleman, and Pizza Hut becoming part of national corporations whose decisions came from offices far away from Wichita. The stockyards closed. Downtown stores faced competition from new malls such as Town West, Town East, and Twin Lakes. Local incidents such as the shooting at the Holiday Inn and the serial killer known as "BTK" gained headlines.

Just as significant was a change in the music industry itself. Venerable mainstays like KFDI and KEYN played a mix of music, from Willie Nelson to Led Zeppelin. The eclectic mix that Randy Crump brought to KMUW continued when he went to work for KFDI in 1977. In 1979, the music market changed when Sanders' FM station became T-95, rebranding itself as a hard rock station, and catapulted itself into the leading position of popular music in Wichita. "It was one of the quickest flips that I ever saw," remembered KFDI's John Speer.

Former site of the Rock Castle, the Hobble-De-Hoi, and the Coyote Club

Former site of the Sound Sircis

Chapter 5
A Generation Grows Up

Through records, the era's iconic 8 tracks, and later, cassettes, mass-produced corporate music could be heard on radios and teenage bedrooms across the country. For the club owner, disco and the DJ became a lucrative alternative to a live band.

In the late 1970s, the live music scene was still big, with bars hosting club bands, regular concerts at Herman Hill Park, bands going out on tour, and musicians coming and going through a bewildering array of groups.

The story of friends Lance Threet, Jerry Sumner, and Gerald Graves illustrates just how complicated these arrangements could be. Sumner and Threet had become friends while at Curtis Junior High. When Threet and Sumner transitioned to Southeast High School, they met up with another young musician, Gerald Graves. Sumner was, at the time, working at King Music where Wayne Roberts of Mr. Roberts and the Rhodesmen/Soule Survivor fame introduced him to the Bacharach and David song *Little Red Book*. By the late 1960s, the three were active in the band scene. Threet and Sumner were founding members of the band Camel. When that band broke up in 1971, Sumner went on to play first in Soldier and later, with Bo Mitchell and Easy Money. Threet went on to play with CLA and later Gandalf. By 1974, Gandalf had transitioned into Lickety Split, the house band for the Stage Door Inn, with Sumner now as drummer. Lickety Split only lasted a short time and by 1975, Threet and Sumner were again together, this time in the band Polite Force. By late 1977, as Threet recalled, "that broke up when Kevin Jones joined the Wumblies and Jeff (Stevenson) moved to California, and Jerry and I ended up in Sir Cuss for a short time." Joining them in Sir Cuss was keyboardist Gerald Graves, who had embarked on his own local music career, playing in Majestic Mood and later, with Tin Ear.

Graves, Sumner, and Threet had a different vision of the band from those of the founding members, however. Sumner remembered that, "we wanted to go on the road. It seems Bally (Larry) and (Jim) Quincy didn't want to" and, according to Threet, "Jerry, Gerald and I moved on from Sir Cuss, we took on

Courtesy: The Clocks

Paul Slagle (bass) and the Polite Force name again." This was in the late 1970s. For a time, a number of musicians came and went, but by 1979, Polite Force, version two, had gained drummer Todd Hidden, who had played with Sumner back in the days of Soldier and of Bo Mitchell and Easy Money. When Hidden left, the band brought in Steve Swaim, who had played with Threet in CLA and Gandalf. As a club band, the group became known for a new sound, that of the New Wave. The group also toured and, in anticipation of a tour up to Canada, decided on a name change to become the Clocks. As the Clocks, the group began gaining more local attention and then made a recording, including a version of *Little Red Book* that inspired them, to go to Los Angeles to record.

Out in California, the group recorded at Sound City Studio in Van Nuys under the guidance of Mike Flicker, who had produced for Heart and other groups. It was then that an earlier time when Cheap Trick showed up to Tennessee Gin Mill became a stroke of fate. Threet recalled the story on the blog, thecollegecrowddigsme.com: "Cheap Trick's guitarist Rick Nielsen was in the A & R office at Epic Records. And this guy's talking to him, 'Hey, have ya seen anybody cool lately?' And he said, 'Yeah. I seen (sic) a band in Wichita that had some pretty good original songs.' Guy started quizzing him about us and he said, 'Wait a minute. (Opens drawer of a desk and takes tape out.) 'You mean these guys?' Rick said, 'Oh yeah, I think that's them.' That's kind of how the ball got rolling. Just on a fluke, y'know?" That Wichita band, the Clocks, had a hit, "She Looks a Lot Like You," in 1982 with a video that was featured on MTV, helping pioneer what was just starting to emerge as a musical genre.

Back in Wichita, however, other bands struggled with the changes in rock music. The demands for televised music were even more intense than in the hard rock era, when the bands simply had to play loud or put on a show. Creating music videos required a whole new set of skills and financing. There was more involved than aiming a camera at a live audience. A local band might be great, but they can't compete with Van Halen.

Then, came the launching of MTV. MTV

and the cable music industry completely transformed how America's youth got their music. Young people could watch it on TV or listen to it individually on their Walkmans. The live scene was slowing down. There were more varieties to choose from and the glamorous world of a Madonna or a Journey did not hold up to a small club in Wichita. The youth music of the 1960s and 1970s was becoming "classic

> "We really tried but eventually we went to work for Boeing."
> – Curtis Payne

rock." Raucous baby boomers who challenged the system were growing up into more responsible adults with careers and homes. It was not by coincidence that the 1980s saw a wave of nostalgia, especially for the 1950s and early 1960s, as baby boomers started to recall the decades of their childhood. Nationally, movies like *Back to the Future* celebrated the 1950s as a golden era of innocence, before the turmoil of the 1960s and 1970s. Restaurant chains like Spangles recreated gleaming Route 66 diners complete with Elvis memorabilia and rockabilly record covers on the walls.

During the grind, bands and musicians tried to keep up with the music, from the Beatles to glam rock, to hard rock to country rock. Now, musicians and their fans went back to the classics. The Jackson Browne song "Stay" may have been partially responsible for an oldies revival as well as the movie the Big Chill. Groups like Red Shirt, the Fun Tones, the Del Reys, and the Dive Kings played 1950s and 1960s music in the 1980s. Teenagers who grew up enjoying live rock & roll now had venues like the West Bank Stage and Riverfest concerts where the whole family could attend. As young adults settled down and became successful, they found themselves able to

Courtesy: The Dive Kings

indulge their passion for rock as a hobby. Some had done very well, as when entrepreneur Tom Devlin could afford to bring in the Beach Boys for one birthday party.

The Dive Kings were one of the most popular bands from the era and also showed how much things had shifted. Featuring Jim Hill and Curtis Payne on guitar, Larry Bally on drums, Phil Nelson on bass, Bob Gilbert on Hammond B-3, Michael Penny on saxophone, Kate Nelson on trumpet, and Patrick "Cigs" Jennings as lead vocal, the Dive Kings formed in the late 1970s, first performing at the Swedish Buffet about 1978. Their members cut their teeth in Wichita's 3.2 club scene. They had had their wild side and called themselves "Wichita's Second Favorite Party Band," because Dewy and the Big Dogs claimed the title of being the "Favorite Party Band." Now, however, the musicians were a little older with families and jobs, just like their audience. They still had an edge but were also part of the local mainstream: In 1981, they debuted at the New Year's party at the Broadview Hotel. Another of their early gigs was at a Pizza Hut pool party hosted at the Wichita Country Club. Eventually, the Dive Kings partnered with KAKE TV to become that station's "family band," playing at events like Riverfest.

The Dive Kings opened for Riverfest in 1986, just weeks after KKRD 107.3 Radio assembled the "Big Reunion Show" at Century II. This event brought together some of the biggest names in local music including The Board of Regents and Mike Finnigan. Red Shirt acted as the house band for the event and backed The Soule Survivors and Mike Finnigan that evening. This show was both a celebration of rock music and a sign that things had changed as musicians were starting to look back on their youth. It resonated with a generation that was itself getting older and becoming more respectable.

Music had always been a business as well as a passion and several musicians turned their love of rock into a career by supporting rock musicians. Thesis and Sahara benefitted from the skills of Mike Metz, who founded Thesis Audio, a company specializing in the repair of musical equipment. Doug Adams knew from his time with Bandit and Sweetwater that being a professional musician was a very difficult career. He found, however, that being behind the scenes was also rewarding and that sound production enabled him to "take a group of five people and make one instrument." Adams began working as a sound man for Oklahoma Sunshine as well as, The Clocks, Dogs? and many others, resulting in the creation of Pro Audio Systems, Inc., a firm that provided light, sound and technical support to touring rock bands. Since 1989, Adams has been the stage manager and sound engineer for John Kay & Steppenwolf.

Richard Lamb followed a similar course, creating Speak House Audio before leaving that business and devoting his career to hosting a radio and television show dedicated to horse enthusiasts. A few, like Jim Hill, kept playing, at first taking jobs at music stores during the day to supplement his income. In 1986, Hill went to work for Senseney Music, a business that focused on music education, supplying resources for music instructors, as well as offering instruments, and instrument repair. Hill created the store's guitar department. Meanwhile, Clif Major opened his own music business in 1978. For nearly 35 years, until it closed in 2012, C Major Guitars & Banjos was well-known for its vintage guitars and equipment and later live music venues but also a place where people could come and jam. The sign for C Major Guitars, also known as a music venue called C Major Rockin' Daddy's, had become a fixture at Douglas and Hillside Avenues.

Others transitioned into being club owners, as did Don Overstake when he acquired the Fireside and later, Margarita's. Overstake had long lamented that "Wichita doesn't eat where it parties and doesn't party where it eats." When he set up Margarita's Cantina, he was able to realize that vision of that club he saw in Texas where people could eat a meal and enjoy live music. Margarita's was one of the last local venues that still employed a regular house band-- Lotus. Wichita's longest lasting live bands, Lotus experienced an amazing stream of local talent such as Martina McBride, before her move to country music. Others played only for a short time, including Pat McJimsey, who had played with Lotus at a special concert at the Cotillion.

Courtesy: Ron Starkel

Danny Loveland, meanwhile, continued operating the club Carats, changing it into Traks, a roller-skating rink in 1980, only to transform it again the following year into "Backstage," the largest 3.2 nightclub in Kansas at the time. He eventually sold Backstage in 1983 and a few years later, left the music business entirely, becoming an entrepreneur in Thailand.

A significant number of band musicians did well in business, allowing them to continue their music careers on the side. Long haired young men who partied hard in the 1970s had, by the 1980s, cleaned up their appearance and become attorneys and accountants. Others went into the family business, or founded businesses of their own. One such story began in the late 1970s, when a group of friends came together to form a band called Storm. These young men were in high school and after college, went their separate ways. In 1982, these friends came back to Wichita to begin their work careers but never lost the love for rock music. Several members, including some from Storm, formed the basis of a new group that came to include Dave Clothier, Randy Rathbun, Clay Bastian, George Van Riper; Larry Beck, Mick Haugen, Alan Banta, Clark Engbrecht, and Mike "Mad Dog" Fleming. Initially just a jam session where musicians could play "1960s music with a punk attitude." When asked about the band's name, an off-hand joke was that they were "The Fabulous Shitheads." The name stuck and even respectable audiences referred to the band by that name, in spite of attempts to change it. Officially for publicity, it was sometimes referred to as the "Shi(r)theads. Banta has mused about why so many of his peers were both successful business figures and enthusiastic rockers. He wondered whether the need for rock bands to operate like a business instilled an entrepreneurial sense of many young rockers as they grew older. Since the 1950, the most successful bands had to make the leap and transitioned from just groups of musicians into organized ventures with general managers who could book gigs and maintained the finances. Looking back on his life, Hal Davis of Solomon and the Monarchs mused that "I had more spare change then than I do now."

Those who continued to perform professionally looked to figures like musician, writer, and producer John Salem for help. Working at studios such as Hi Fidelity and Big Dog in Wichita, as well as Ironside in Branson, Salem provided support for a wide range of groups during the 1980s. His contributions shaped and guided the music careers from Rudy Love, Dwayne Bailey, Pat McJimsey, and Jerry Hahn to The Embarrassment, Dewy and the Big Dogs, The James Brothers, and the Macy Brothers.

Scores of other musicians went to work for the aircraft industry, professionals, education, medicine, or any number of regular occupations. Some were able to continue to play with friends. Still others drifted, or moved, or simply burned out, reliving the glory of those rock years, going through photos and albums.

Along with the musicians, the club and music scene was changing as well. In part this was due to changing tastes and the decline of live music. Another reason was the changing of liquor laws. Nationwide, the legal drinking age changed from 18 to 21, cutting a whole segment of the youth market out of the bar trade. In Kansas, liquor by the drink arrived in 1987, ending the need for clubs to charge memberships. With that, restaurants across the city could serve alcohol, ending the need for special clubs. A new wave of bars and clubs down in "Old Town" used DJs, not live music, to draw customers.

One by one, the clubs started to go. The Penthouse became the University Club, then a bank. It then became part of Wichita State University and now houses a center for international studies. On north Broadway, the Rock Castle complex that had operated since 1935 had gone through many names and incarnations. In 1977, Art Busch, grandson of the original founders, took it over as the Coyote Club. It hosted local and traveling bands that played everything from rock to blues to

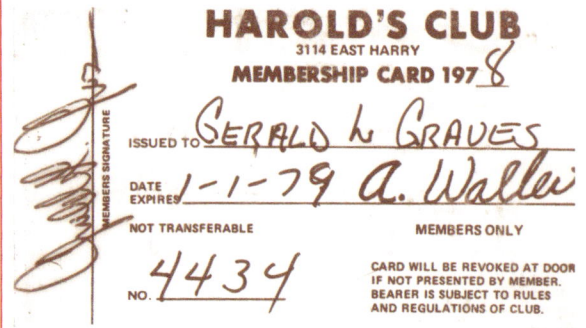

country, from obscure locals to the Red Hot Chili Peppers. A local landmark, the Coyote Club was not a money maker and in 1993, Busch closed the club's doors. Gage Brewer's Shadowland went through many incarnations to become the property of the Church of God in Christ, who reworked it into a religious facility.

Meanwhile, local rock music continued to evolve. In 1984, for example, a group of high school friends from Norwich, Kansas, came together to form a band. The original lineup was Tim Heuback, John Raida and John Coykendall. In 1985, Coykendall mailed a cassette of home recordings to the KMUW After Midnight program. The name written on the cassette was Klyde Konnor and this, for a time, became the

Courtesy: The Fabulous Shitheads

band's name. Coykendall recalled that "the name was a re-spelling of a neighbor's name who always came over to ask them to stop playing. Known as a "three piece prairie-psych band," Klyde Konnor recorded a single "What's She Doin' with Him" in 1985 and, the following year, a full-length cassette release titled *The Weaker the Stronger*. Playing music that ranged from The Beatles to Pink Floyd, they performed at Kirby's, The Spot, and The B-1 Club. However, the group wanted to remain experimental, a sound that did not always agree with audiences. In 1986, they received the accolade of "best band in Kansas" by the *Wichita Eagle and Beacon*. Two years later, they received the dubious "worst live band" designation in the Gopher Purge music magazine. The group eventually found a compromise: performing pop music under Klyde Konnor while releasing more experimental sounds under the alter-ego of The Tangle Brains. In 1991, Klyde played their last official show and recorded (in one day) "When Worlds Klyde." Coykendall then relocated to San Francisco.

Klyde Konnor was just one of a new set of bands including Joe's Nose, Roach Egg Invasion, Winking Spaniard, Nervous Pudding, The Blivets, Technicolor Headrush, and The Sluggos. As the 1980s became the 1990s, a number of these groups fused rock with folk, country, and punk to form the basis of a new alternative scene. Groups like Split Lip Rayfield, with their fusion of blues, bluegrass, folk, and rock, have gained local, regional, and national acclaim. It is a different scene than the Teen Bunny Club, the 3.2 Bars, and battles of the bands, but the passion remains.

Rock in Wichita has continued as a new crop of teenagers learned the techniques of those who had starting playing back during the days of the battles of the bands. For many years, Clif Major's guitar studio at Hillside and Douglas was a local music hangout. Heading west on Douglas stood Margarita's, where Lotus continued as the house band. West of Margarita's near East High stood EM Shorts Guitars. Across the street from East High on Douglas stood Phil Uhlik Music, which had supported the local music scene since the 1960s. A musician heading just a short distance south on Grove would find Senseney Music, where individuals like Jim Hill conveyed the legacy of the 1960s and 1970s to a new generation. These efforts

Courtesy of the Wichita-Sedgwick County Historical Museum

have paid off. It was just such a group of young rock musicians who played at the opening gala for a joint exhibit on the electric guitar co-hosted by the Wichita-Sedgwick County Historical Museum and Exploration Place, an event that also featured a performance by Jerry Hahn. Here, with guitars such as those of Wichita native Joe Walsh on display, Wichita's rock legacy lived on, the newest expression of this colorful part of Wichita's heritage.

Former site of the King Cole Inn

Former site of the Colony Club

Part Two:
Wichita Band Gallery

This research project tried to identify the major rock bands and musicians who performed in Wichita between the late 1950s and middle 1980s. As part of the process, the team had to make some decisions. In general, a band had to have played in public more than once or twice to be considered. Solo musicians are discussed in both the main text and among the band biographies here but did not get their own entries. The main focus was on bands that performed in Wichita which meant that we did not cover bands that were from or played in Hutchinson, El Dorado, Wellington, or other locales unless there was a significant connection to Wichita. In some cases, the team decided to combine the story one or more bands into a single entry, especially if the groups were made up of essentially the same performers or one band renamed itself. To make the listing manageable, the team decided to not include bands from the middle 1980s on unless most of the members were active during the 1950-1980 period. Moreover, the post 1980s era was a different music scene with different influences. It is one that is currently attracting the attention of a different group of researchers who will, hopefully, continue the work done here to explore the next generation of the local music story.

Even within these parameters, however, tracking down bands and performers has been both an adventure and a challenge. It has involved holding gatherings at Margarita's, posting articles in the newspaper, maintaining a Facebook page, researching back issues of old newspaper editions, scouring websites and YouTube entries, and managing an ever growing number of phone calls, letters, emails, interviews, and informal conversations. It has been a time consuming process. Several times, the team thought they were finishing up only to discover a whole new crop of bands and musicians and the process had to start over.

The goal was to be as thorough as possible but the team knew that some bands would get overlooked or not get the coverage they deserved. The project team regrets not being able to tell the stories of groups like Band-o-matic, Cockyfox, Desert Wind, Effigy, Jericho, The John Hancock Band, Medusa, Richard Walters and the Aristocrats, Roanoke, and the Soul Kings among others. There were scores of club bands, small bands, high school and middle school bands, and others who are not listed and several that probably deserve full listings. Some were known among circles of friends, some were little more than a name, and others were exactly the opposite." In some cases, a few names of band members were known but the story was too incomplete to create a fill entry. The team also knows that there are individuals who played with the bands listed who are not mentioned, perhaps because they played for a short time or were part of only one part of a band's story. The project team apologizes in advance for these oversights and welcomes any additional information. This book is not the end of the story. It is just the start.

The Wileys

Milo Wiley opened a small music store in Wichita in the mid-1930s and specialized in steel guitars. When a sales rep came into the store with electric guitars from a new company called Fender, Wiley was thrilled. In 1947, the store was one of the country's first Fender dealers.

Throughout his childhood Bobby Wiley played music. He played steel guitar before there were pedal steel guitars. Bobby went on to design his own guitars over the years and remained a well-respected leader in the industry. By 1953, Bobby already was a veteran performer, billed as "Bob Wiley, 13-year-old steel guitar wizard" by local music promoter Hap Peebles. Band members were lead guitar

Jerry Hahn; Bob Smith – who played both bass and fiddle; Bobby's cousin, Diane Hamilton, as a vocalist; and drummer Mac McKenzie. The youngest member was 11-year old Bernie Rozell, who played rhythm guitar and sang.

Photos Courtesy: Carol Wiley

Courtesy: Tom Wise

The Rock-N-Tones

The Rock-N-Tones formed in 1956 with Ed Macy on guitar; Jerry Hahn on guitar, Don Wise, piano and brother Bob Wise on drums. One of the first, if not the first rock bands in Wichita, they played venues from the Stardust to the Trig to the Pirate's Cove. Other band members included J R. Tunison and Junior Prather.

The band's career came to an end when front man Don Wise was paralyzed in a swimming accident in 1961.

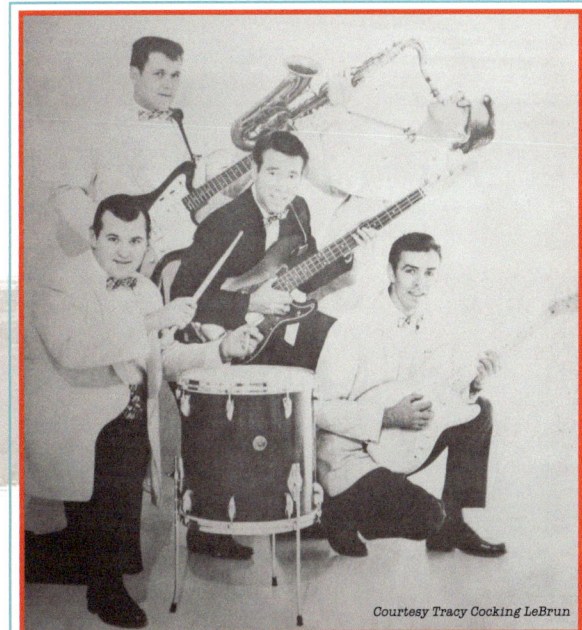

Courtesy Tracy Cocking LeBrun

The Premieres

It was 1957 and a young Bucky Walters had just graduated from East High ready to start classes at the University of Wichita. While there, he and two classmates formed a band called The Premieres. At first, the lineup was Bucky Walters, front man and vocals; John Holt, guitar, and Gary Cocking on drums, with other players coming in and out of the group. The main three realized they needed a saxophonist and another guitarist, putting out an ad in the paper for these roles. As a result, the group added Carlis Cassle on saxophone and Tony Caire on guitar. Gene Humphrey, who ran Nu Phi Records, was the band manager. The band recorded several 45s including the first 45 recorded on red vinyl. The Premiers started to play local gigs, including playing in connection with KFBI. They got a gig playing at Joyland with Chuck Berry, whose lack of rehearsing and challenging attitude made for a less than ideal experience. Two weeks later, the Premieres played Joyland again to front for Jerry Lee Lewis. Lewis did not show up but the agent had booked Floyd Robinson. In a hasty reorganization, Joyland advertized Floyd Robinson and the Premieres. Joyland was relieved, as was their agent, T.B. Skarning, who began booking them to tour, as needed, to support his other clients, most notably the Johnny Cash Show. This was in 1959.

The next year, the Premieres decided to try some touring of their own, acquiring a trailer for their equipment. En route to a gig in Austin, Minnesota, the trailer came off and wrecked. The band tried to salvage their equipment and toured as best they could. In between touring, the band members tried to maintain their studies at Wichita University. The next year, the Premieres set out again this time, with Jerry Hahn on guitar and Johnny Chiccarelli on drums. Walters also filled in to play bass as well as vocals. They toured from Arkansas to Minnesota, sometimes playing dance clubs and also supper clubs—where their main role was background music. By the early 1960s, Walters was looking to settle down into a career and found himself in beauty school, much to the amazement of T.B. Skarning, who continued to call and offer gigs. In the meantime, Walters played with a short-lived group called The Tradewinds that, at times included Fred Bonner, Jerry Wood, and Tom Castleberry.

Courtesy: Fred Bonner

Courtesy: KWCH

Rhythm Rousers

Donn Salyer, a keyboard player who performed with the Chuck Dooling Band, helped organize a group of middle school students into an accordion/rock band in the late 1950s and early 1960s. One poster proclaimed: Follow The Crowd to the Rockin'est Band Around!! the "RHYTHM 'ROUSERS." Performing at Hi Fi Hop, the 20th Century Club, and other events, the band included Gail Cauthon, Bob Garvey, Dennis Cauthon, and Larry Kelly on guitar and Dale Davis on drums. guitar, and Larry Kelly on guitar.

Tiny Lyman and the Jukes

His real name is Homer McMinn, better known now as Papa Don McMinn, a regular performer on Beale Street since the 1980s.

He made a 45, "Mary Jane," in the 1960s on the Runnin' Wild label as Tiny Lyman & the Jukes.

The Jukes were Don on guitar, F.J. Seitz on drums, Bobby Marquiz on bass and Jerry Wood on Saxophone.

McMinn also had a later single with Dee Dee Ford called "I Can't Stand It."

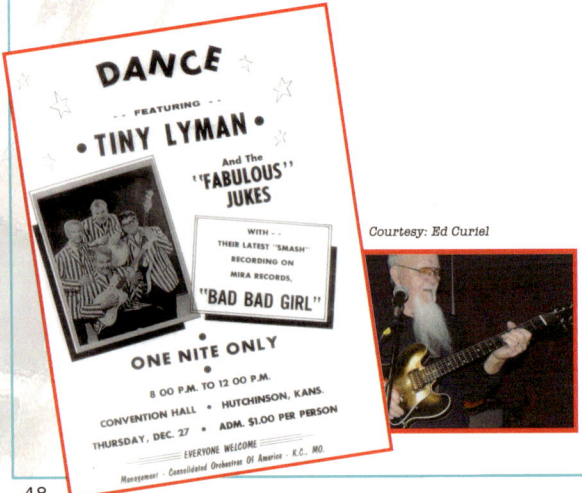

Dennis Hunt & the Hunters

Courtesy: Dennis Hunt

It was a November night in 1959 at The Gardens in Wichita that Eddie Cochran played his last one-nighter before leaving the U.S. on his final personal appearance tour. "Somethin' Else" made it up to No. 3 on KSIR, the local radio station. Dennis Hunt, the local teen DJ and rocker was a real Cochran fan. He always sang Eddie's songs at the Saturday night sock hops and, as expected, he was the host of the Eddie Cochran Show. Hunt, singing in a very Elvis-like style, entertained for approximately an hour before The Hollywood Swingers took over.

Carlos Castle, sax; Dennis Hunt, guitar; Fred Bonner, drums; Tony Caire, guitar.

The Tone Twisters

Courtesy: The Tone Twisters

Doug Trowbridge, guitar; Jim Kent, sax; John Chambers, guitar; Orby Brown, drums.

The top picture was taken at the old Southern movie theatre that later became The Stagedoor and is today a VFW. They were in 8th grade and played a couple of songs between movies.

The Ravens

The house band for the Green Onion between 1962 and 1963, the Ravens consisted of Jim Swingley on bass and lead vocals, Larry Kelly on lead guitar, Gary Smith on drums, and Paul Railing on sax. According to one recollection, they were all south enders and played strictly the hits of the day—Beatles, Gerry and the Pacemakers, and Herman's Hermits etc."

The Debonaires / Keys

One of the members of the The Debonaires, Tom Beard, formed a group called the Keys that consisted of Beard as leader (and keyboardist); Larry Hurst, bass and vocals; and Johnny Holt, Don Tunison and Jerry Hahn, guitar. There were several individuals who played drums including Jim Black and Tommy Hernandez. Of part Native American ancestry, Black was famous for announcing "I'm Jimmy Carl Black, and I'm the Indian of the group."

Coming out of the 1950s, they played rock inspired by figures such as Bill Haley and the Comets. Because Beard had a job servicing juke boxes around town, both he and the band were able to hear and learn the newest and latest songs. In 1962, they recorded a 45 record with the song "Stretch Pants" on one side and "Just a Matter of Time" on the other.

The group only lasted a few years and most members went on to other careers and endeavors. Some members of the group, however, continued to perform music. The most prominent was Jimmy Carl Black, who went on to form the group Geronimo Black and, most famously, played drums for Frank Zappa's Mothers of Invention.

Gentleman J and the Goodtimes

The name of the band was Gentleman J and the Goodtimes, which for a time was the house band for the Red Dog Inn (the other major house band being that of Mike Finnigan). They also toured, however, working with the band at Ft. Riley, the Newman center at WSU, Dwayne Zambo's Zoo downtown, and the Miss Kansas Pageant in Pratt, among others.

The band started when Norman Lee decided that he would try some rock & roll on one of his 'Norman Lee Orchestra' gigs. Norman hired Jerry Spohn and Mickey Sheaks to play with the Orchestra. One evening, Lee announced that the band would take a break and that Spohn and Sheaks would play some rock & roll. The two looked at each other and quickly corralled Doris Buss, the keyboard player and her husband Leonard, the bass player. They played until the band came back from break. This was the band's annual drunk event and it showed.

By the late 1960s, Lee, Sheaks, and Spohn were not working much. Wayne Roberts of Mr. Roberts and the Rhodesmen contacted Sheaks and asked him to come back with that group at the Green Onion that was working six nights a week. He needed the money and returned with the Rhodesmen while Gentleman J and the Goodtimes hired Danny Personne to replace Sheaks on drums.

Later on, the band added two female singers, who formed the basis of a side group called The Rye. Eventually, MidContinent entertainment managed the group, but under the name Spider and the Crabs, featuring The Rye.

Berry Harris

Originally from Chockie, Oklahoma, Berry Harris joined a band in Muskogee, Oklahoma, after returning from serving overseas in the army. By the late 1950s, he was in Wichita playing at clubs like the Bomber Club near Boeing, the Tik Tok Club, and a host of African-American clubs like 904, the Mambo Club, and Flagler Gardens.

Playing electric guitar, keyboard, and harmonica, Harris was rooted in the blues scene, Harris was part of generation of African-American musicians who helped the local music scene transition from blues to R&B to rock.

He became a mainstay in groups like "The Jive Five" (not to be confused with a Brooklyn-based group of the same name). Through the 1970s until disco and disc jockeys limited opportunities for live bands. Reflecting on his life and his music, he said "I ain't been perfect, but I've been good."

Courtesy: Berry Harris

The Imperials

The Imperials were an in-demand soul band from Hutchinson. They played all over the region and also appeared regularly at the Fireside on 30th Ave. in Hutchison, one of the hottest night spots in Kansas. It featured local, regional and national acts.

Their lineup included Ralph Brown on sax/flute; Kenny Hill was vocalist, Gary LeClair, guitar; Gayland Bland, trumpet; Ray Wiggins on B3 organ; Jim Frick, bass; and Ed Curiel on drums. Other members were Odell Reed, vocals; Mike D'Robertus, guitar, and Geniva Hawthorne Robinson on vocals.

Photos courtesy of: Ed Curiel

The Squires

Photos courtesy: Jim Wood

Tom Green, guitar; Gary Stephens, organ; Jack Skinner, bass; Jim Wood, drums. Popular and busy, the Squires played all over—Dearmores, the Hi Ho, Stardust, Rock Castle, the Seneca Lounge and P.J.'s. They played six nights a week at The Seneca Lounge until midnight, and then went to the Esquire Club to play until 4 a.m. on Friday and Saturday. They moved to Denver and opened shows for Sonny & Cher, Johnny Rivers and Jimmy Reed.

Courtesy: The Echoes

The Echoes

Formed in the early 1960s, the Echoes went through two versions. The first version was made up of several members of the Tone Twisters. By 1962, the band consisted of Doug Trowbridge, guitar; John Chambers, guitar; Rick Howell, piano; Dennis Burns, drums; and Jim Kent on saxophone. They did Sunday afternoon teen dances at the Hi Ho and other venues on the city's north side and south sides.

By 1963, a new version of the band had come together. It included John Chambers, Tom Green, Dennis Burns, and Bob 'Kingfish" King on bass.

Photos courtesy: Ed Curiel

Jerry Wood and the Peggs

Ed Curiel drums; Joe Martinez, guitar; bassist Galen Sickler; and Wood on guitar, keyboards, sax and harmonica.

The way drummer Ed Curiel heard the story was that some tall, skinny kid walked up to the stage at a Tiny Lyman and the Jukes gig and asked for an audition. The request was granted and Jerry Wood was hired on the spot.

This would come as no surprise to the lucky Wichita teens that just a few years earlier had the opportunity to hear this phenomenal talent perform at the KiddieLand outdoor pavilion on summer nights in the late 1950s.

In Kansas City, word spread fast about the Jukes' new lineup with the band belting out flawless renditions of James Brown and Ray Charles tunes. They had a steady gig at The Carousel Club. B.B. King played across the street.

When Lyman left the Jukes, Wood soldiered on with the Jukes as a trio—Bobby Marquez on bass and Frank "FJ" Seitz on drums. Returning to Wichita, Wood joined The Peggs with Ron Kissac on drums and Gaylen Sickler on bass, soon Ed Curiel was drafted into as the Peggs' new drummer.

Six nights a week The Peggs performed to large crowds at Dearmore's and played a regular gig at Meadowlake Beach on Sundays. Often, after Dearmore's closed for the night, The Peggs would join Mike Finnigan and other musicians for after-hour's jam sessions at the Aladdin Club that lasted well into the early hours.

Charlie Daniels heard the Peggs at Meadowlake Beach and was so impressed he got them signed with his agent Bill Sizemore at Interstate Artists Corp. out of Lexington, Ky.

The band performed across the Midwest and eastern seaboard. Ruby Winters was added as lead vocalist and the band was scheduled to record at King Records studio in Cincinnati. However, before the date arrived, Wood canceled for personal reasons.

During this period, Wood moved to Ark City and later back to Wichita and continued to play around the area.

Courtesy: The Jags

The Jags

Johnny Chambers on B-3, Vern Harris on bass, Richard Hepner on guitar, Dolph Ybarra on sax and Bob Suttle on drums.

Hailing from Wellington, the Jags started at the "It'll Do Club". They entertained youngsters from Blackwell, Winfield, Ark City and South Wichita.

The Jags made their way to Denver and ultimately Las Vegas, headlining the Vegas Strip. The members changed, but Ybarra and Little were mainstays. Little's life as a professional drummer continued, playing countless shows with notable musicians, including Frank Sinatra.

The Serfs

Word of mouth traveled fast in the summer of 1964. The hottest news burning up Wichita's musical grapevine was concerning a new house band playing at Dearmore's—a basement 3.2 beer tavern— across from the Coca-Cola bottling plant. The band was called the "Serfs," but on first reference, most people heard the "Surfs." A more radical misinterpretation of the spelling and definition could not be imagined. Those expecting heavy reverb and triple-picking Fender guitars were greatly mistaken and instead introduced to a fantastic roadhouse rhythm & blues band fronted by vocal powerhouse Mike Finnigan.

The Serfs became the yardstick by which all other bands were measured. With the bar set high, Wichita bands became better musicians from the listening experience. In fact, Finnigan tutored some local bands with his keen ear, great musicianship and musical knowledge.

While many players graced the stage of the Serfs over the years, the one constant was the soulful voice of Finnigan. The Serfs were a mainstay of the Wichita music scene until the late '60s when Finnigan moved his base of operations to California. Over the years, his recording and touring credentials reads like a who's who of the music industry.

Mike Finnigan was inducted into the Kansas Music Hall of Fame in 2005.

The Pendulums

The Pendulums included Dan Cunningham, lead guitar; Larry Chambers, bass; Greg Peterson, rhythm guitar; Dan Chambers, keyboard and lead vocals, and Kerry Baker, drums. The group never liked its name, but chose it because they received a professionally-painted "Swing with Pendulums" banner, featuring a pendulum swinging from a clock. They decided they couldn't afford an expensive banner so they concluded: "What's in a name?"

The Pendulums focused on playing high-energy rock and roll that included top-40 hits. The band played high school dances, CYO dances, private parties, even pizza restaurants and swim-club gigs. They also won a few 'battle of the bands competitions.

The Pendulums were a true 'garage band'– practicing in Cunningham's garage. After months of listening to nightly band practice, neighborhood dogs had perfected every popular dance. The group disbanded when members left for college or began to pursue other career interests.

The Smart Brothers

Courtesy: The Smart Brothers

Smart's Palace, a night club owned by the Smart family, was the epicenter of the Wichita Kansas soul scene between 1963 and 1975. The Smart Brothers (there were eight of them) formed the Smart Brothers Band, and held court there.

Touring acts such as James Brown and Aretha Franklin would often sit in with the group. By all accounts, their shows were animated and wild affairs, featuring front men John and Leroy Smart. Popping handstands and jumping from table to table in the club while soloing were just a few of the acrobatics featured in a typical show.

At the heart of the organization was Dick Smart. As, bassist, club and record store owner, DJ, Promoter, and all around businessman, he also formed Solo Records. Recordings for the label featuring various Smart Brothers band lineups are featured on the 2009 Numero Records CD compilation "Eccentric Soul: Smart's Palace". The Smart Brothers were inducted into the Kansas Music Hall of Fame in 2016.

The Downbeats

The Downbeats were a popular rock & roll band from Wichita who played clubs and concert venues in Kansas, Oklahoma and Nebraska from 1963-70. The band was started by guitarists Gary Bolen, Marty Ford and Barry Sigars, drummer John Bowman, vocalist Jim Holmes, and organist John Clampitt. Eventually, they hired bass player Mike Brittain. In '64, organist Don Sailing replaced John Clampitt.

After Mike Brittain left in '66, the band hired Dave and Lanny Gaston on horns. This six man group played several years together, recording an original single, "Trying To Get Through" with the flip side a cover of the Len Barry hit, "1- 2- 3". This record led to their audition for a Hollywood talent show in '68 called "The All American College Show." A video of the performance can be seen at *www.the downbeats all american college show. youtube.*

Besides opening for the McCoys, The Grass Roots, The Ohio Express, and Brian Hyland, they provided the backup music for B J Thomas at the Go Mod Revue in '69.

At various times in '69, they hired guitarists Wayne Avery, Mike Musick, and Gary Heitz. In 1970, The Downbeats disbanded, but had a reunion in 2000, booking new gigs and playing the same great '60s music they played years earlier.

Photos: The Downbeats

The Outcasts

Photos courtesy: Mark Archibald

Membership in the Outcasts changed frequently with one constant factor—guitarist Clif Major. An edgy and innovative musician, Major had an uncanny knack for attracting topnotch musicians, which resulted in a strong fan-base regardless of the roster.

In the early days following the British Invasion, competition between Wichita bands was fierce. Major was fond of recalling how words became heated between the Outcasts and another local band, whose name is lost to history. The rivals—as the story goes—decided to "duke it out" after school in some deserted parking lot. The bands met, circled each other sizing up the opposing combatants. Sullen and snarly, before the first punch could be landed, the conversation turned to guitars, amps and the latest musical hits. The two bands talked music and parted company.

In the late '60s, the Outcasts were regularly seen at Sunday concerts in Riverside or Herman Hill parks as well as gigs at the Phone Booth and the Stage Door Inn. Clif Major was inducted into the Kansas Music Hall of Fame in 2014.

Courtesy: Margie Watson

The Group

In 1964, a group of musicians formed in Wellington at the home of Leland and Margie Watson. They included Margie Watson on keyboard, Roger Empty on saxophone and guitar, Little Lee Watson on drums, Leon "Crutch" Crutchfield on lead guitar, and Steve Hartley on bass. They played well together but had no official name other than "the Group." They became one of the main house bands for the Flame Club that opened on Seneca, where they played regularly Mondays, Tuesdays, Fridays and Saturdays. Influenced by the Motown sound, band members finished their gigs at the Flame and then went to jam with African-American blues clubs like the 904. The band played until financial problems caused the Flame to close in 1965.

Danny Loveland

Danny Loveland started playing with Richard Walters and the Aristocrats at the Flame in 1964. Then Mr. Roberts and the Rhodesmen, a band from Colorado Springs, followed by The Renegades. When the Penthouse opened in June 1966, the house band, the Centurions, included former Renegade members Steve Bowersox on bass guitar, Loveland on drums, John Vawter on guitar, and Alvin Eaton on guitar. Scott Russ on the Hammond organ replaced Eaton soon after. In 1968, the group recorded the record "Spicks and Specks" under the name "Blue Banana" on the Kanwic Label. In 1969, the Penthouse band recorded a second single, "The End of the World," on the Happy Tiger label under the name Danny Loveland and the Luv Bugs.

In 1969, Loveland opened his own club, the "Draftboard" located in the former Green Onion location, but returned to the Penthouse three months later. In 1970, he joined Royal Flush, the house band for the newly-opened club, Casino, but soon left to form the band Shagnasty for the sole purpose of going to California. Shagnasty included Dick Parsley on organ; Greg Dunn on guitar, keyboards, and drums; Dave Riggins on bass guitar and guitar; and Loveland on drums. In 1972, Shagnasty disbanded and Loveland joined Bo Donaldson and the Heywoods. Later in 1974, Loveland returned to Wichita to be part of Mr. Boogie and the Disco Factory, a venue consisting of a DJ, Loveland as drummer, and a light show, concussion bombs, and speakers. The group's best known event was a concert on Easter weekend of 1974 at Lake Cheney. In 1975, Peggy Rogers at Dick Clark Productions, asked Loveland to return to California to form a new band called Loveland.

By 1978, however, Loveland was back in Wichita and opened "Carats Palladium," the largest teenage Disco in Kansas, complete with "Carats Palladium Saturday Night" on television. In 1980, Loveland changed Carats into Traks, a roller skating rink, only to transform it again the following year into "Backstage," the largest 3.2 nightclub in Kansas at the time. He eventually sold Backstage in 1983 and a few years later, left the music business entirely, becoming an entrepreneur in Thailand.

Jay Walker and the Pedestrians

When members of the Wichita band the Prophets learned they weren't the first to lay claim to that name, they decided to tour under the moniker of Jay Walker and the Pedestrians. The band: Phil Black, guitar; Dell Cady, bass; Jim "Mouse" Beggs, drums; and Richard Walters, keyboards. The band toured extensively in Michigan, Ohio and Wisconsin pulling a trailer full of equipment with the bass player's 1958 Volkswagen. The group performed an eclectic mix of British invasion, blues and soul music. The band took special pride in performing the James Brown "Live at the Apollo" album in its entirety.

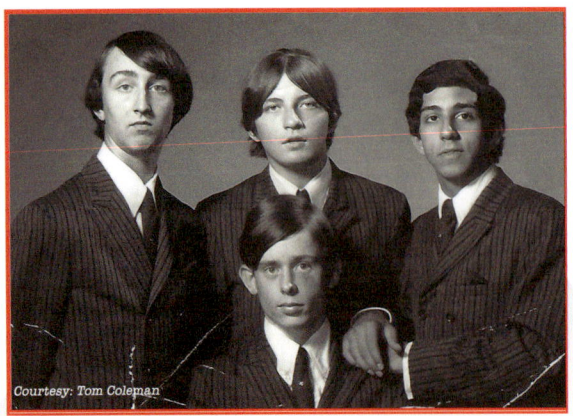
Courtesy: Tom Coleman

The Lion's Mane

Originally formed as a trio of students from Kapaun in 1965, the Lion's Mane was comprised of Greg Skaff, guitar and vocals; Rich Ridder, bass and vocals; and Dan Monnat, drums and vocals. In 1966, the band added Tom Coleman on keyboards and when he departed two years later, he was replaced by Stan Spurrier. Bass player Ridder left the group in 1969. The Prophets played a strong influence in their music as did Mike Finnegan and the Serfs. Finnigan took them under his wing and would come to practice, helping with arrangements and providing records to study. He used to sneak them into the Red Dog/Early Bird Cafe to watch the Serfs.

Courtesy: Dan Monnat

Moanin' Glories

Photos: Courtesy of The Moanin' Glories

A virtual soundtrack to the 1960s, the Moanin' Glories embraced not only the music of the British Invasion, but during their six-year career embraced the heavier album sounds of FM-underground radio.

The band—Ritchie Kunkle, guitar; Andy Gore bass; Karl Berkebile, keyboards; and Marc Mourning, drums—played a rough-styled rhythm and blues much like The Rolling Stones, The Yardbirds and The Animals.

Their road gigs, promoted on Oklahoma City's powerful KOMA-took them throughout the Midwest. Venues varied from high-school dances to National Guard Armories. The band's long hair and sense of fashion got admiring glances from teenage girls, however, this did not always set well with the local boys in attendance. On more than one occasion the band had to make a quick retreat out of town. The Moanin' Glories were inducted into the Kansas Music Hall of Fame in 2010.

The Fabulous Apostles

With the British Invasion in full swing, four high-school students formed the Apostles in the summer of 1964. The original group was comprised of Jay Leach, guitar; Richard Tade, rhythm guitar and later keyboards; Kent Wilson, bass; and Gregg Fuson, drums. Since one of the band's major Wichita rivals was the Prophets, the group selected a name with a similar ring—The Apostles.

By 1966, the bands musical tastes had changed and they opted for a fatter sound that could be provided by adding horns. Setting the sights on being the best, the group added the adjective "Fabulous" to their name and added Randy Loveland, bass, trumpet and vocals; and Jim Salomone, saxophone.

The group was influenced by such national acts as Otis Redding, Aretha Franklin, and Mitch Ryder and the Detroit Wheels; as well as regional acts like the Fabulous Flippers, Spider and the Crabs, and the Red Dogs. The band played from Texas to Canada and Colorado to Missouri and their gigs were announced regularly on the powerful KOMA AM radio.

The Fabulous Apostles played giant ballrooms and roof gardens that were constructed to house the big bands of the 1940s. The group toured in a circa 1950s Brill passenger bus they purchased from a retired Wichita Police Chief. The group was undefeated in their Cotillion Battle of the Bands competitions. Later members included Chris Leason and Roger Walls. The Fabulous Apostles were inducted into the Kansas Music Hall of Fame in 2016.

Photos Courtesy: The Apostles

Courtesy: The Weasels

The Weasels

Formed in 1964, The Weasels featured Jerry Wilson, guitar; Buster Beal, guitar; Jim Cox, bass; David Ellis, vocals; Linsey Cutsinger, drums. Also later featuring Jim Calhoun, bass; Doug "Elkshot" Crespin, Drums; Keith Fry, guitar; Rick Maddux, organ; Amboo Ploy, vocals & harmonica; John Van Sickle, guitar; Wade Williams, bass.

Early on the Weasels played hard rock, Chuck Berry, Stones, etc. but in the late 60s they went to playing all original music in a hard rock vein.

The band played on local TV station channel 12 on "12 a Go Go" in 1966. The Weasels played a Cotillion "Battle of The Bands", winning an opportunity to be the opening act for The Turtles. In 1970, they signed a contract with Soundville Records in Houston and moved there and recorded an album which was never released. The band also did some touring in Texas and New Mexico before returning home which was mentioned in an article in Rolling Stone Magazine.

The Breakers

Photos courtesy: The Breakers

The Vibrations began about 1963 when Bob Garvey put together a band made up of fellow high school musicians. The original lineup included Garvey on guitar, Doug Trowbridge on bass, Paul Railing on saxophone, Doug Carey on rhythm guitar, Greg Salmon on keyboard, and Jim Kincaid, who had just left the Ricochets, on drums. In April 1964, with Phil Black on guitar, the Vibrations recorded two instrumentals, Jet Stream, and Beachhead at Hi Fidelity for the DVB recording company. To simulate waves crashing against the shore for the introduction to "Beachhead," the band placed a microphone inside the bowl of a flushing toilet.

The song received frequent air play on local AM-radio stations such KLEO. Jet Stream was even included on a compilation album released in Europe in the 1980s, and guitarist Phil Black laughingly recalled receiving a $20 royalty check.

In drafting up the initial contracts, Bill Post of DVB found that there was already a group named the Vibrations so the band had to come up with a new name. For a short time, the band performed as Mr. Garvey and the Speed Tones, but in late 1964, changed their name to the Breakers, reflecting the group's surf-inspired persona.

The Breakers were one of the first Wichita proponents of the reverb-laden Surf music genre that swept the nation in the early 1960s. They were a regular attraction at Wichita area teen clubs and high school dances.

Over time, members of the group changed and with it the musical focus as well. By the mid-1960s, with the addition of Chuck Comely, vocals, John Dondlinger, drums and Rick Meyer, horns, the band had reinvented itself into one of the more popular show bands in the area.

Courtesy: the Esquires

The Esquires

Formed about 1965, the Esquires consisted of Chris Pruitt, guitar, keyboards, and vocals; Jim Johnson, lead guitar and vocals; Tom Coleman, bass and vocals; and Steve Sheppard, drums. They were largely influenced by British invasion material, Motown and general soul music. The Esquires played high school dances and proms all around Kansas as well as at local clubs including Dearmore's and the Esquire Club in north Wichita. Tom Coleman remembered when they were setting up at the Esquire Club as the Smart Brothers were tearing down. Leroy Smart pulled Coleman aside and said: "listen son, the secret to this business is to start big and end big because nobody pays much attention in between." In June 1966, the Esquires won one of the earliest Battle of the Bands out at David's Discount Store on East Kellogg. The band broke up in September of 1966. Jim Johnson then played with Harry and the Bushmen, Steve Sheppard undertook a career as a drummer in Las Vegas, and Tom Coleman joined the Lion's Mane as their organist. Chris Pruitt went to college and then medical school.

Harry & the Bushmen

Harry and the Bushman formed in 1965 from a group of friends from Wichita High School Southeast. The original members were Harry Dobbin on guitar and vocals, Bob LaRue on guitar, Ken Bell on bass, J.L. McClure on drums. LaRue was soon replaced by Steve Tippin and in the fall of 1966 Jim Johnson took over the rhythm guitar position from Tippin.

The Bushman, as they were more commonly known, had immediate success as the first Wichita band whose playlist consisted mostly of songs from the new West Coast psychedelic scene. With strong six- and twelve-string guitar work from Dobbin, and vocals from Dobbin and Johnson, the Bushman nailed tunes by the Byrds, Moby Grape, and other California groups. The addition of a professional light show run by Dennis Price added to the psychedelic experience by projecting liquid gels, slides and movies, strobe lights and smoke generators as background to the stage.

In 1968 female vocalist Ann Mitchell joined the Bushman and allowed the addition of songs by the Jefferson Airplane to the songlist. The band became popular on the college circuit playing clubs throughout Kansas. In 1968 J.L. McClure left for college and was replaced by drummer Gregg Phelps. The Bushman disbanded in early 1969.

Left, the Bushmen's first posed photo, 1965. Above, loading out of the gymnasium at Southeast High School.

The Omens

The Omens were put together by Tom Green in late 1965. It consisted of Jim Kent on keys, Bob Suttle on drums and Larry Hart on bass. They played the Hi Ho, the Seneca Lounge, Howard's, and McConnell Air Force Base. In the spring of 1966 they moved to Denver. While in Denver they traded Green for Larry Kelly. The group stayed together until Kent went to Vietnam.

They reformed in 1968. They played at The Phone Booth and were the house band at the original Fireside. During that time Steve Railing took over on drums.

After Larry Hart died he was replaced by Rich Ridder.

The Jokers

The Jokers quickly became a popular band, playing at local clubs and entertainment venues including the Attic, the Workshop, the Bunny Club, the Colony Club, Meadow Lake Beach and was the house band for the Stone Fox. The band included lead singer, Duane Arnold; lead guitar, Steve Wilson; rhythm guitar, Greg Lopez; bass guitar Phil Snow, drums, Doug Lindsay. For a few practices, the band received coaching from local legendary musician Mike Finnigan. A cover band, they became known for their use of props and sound effects on many tunes. Lindsay's grandfather, a former Vaudeville musician, ran the Kansas Music Co. on North Market and was very helpful on using the various effects. Among their effects were boat and bird whistles on "Sittin' on the Dock of the Bay," hitting a trash can lid hit with timpani mallets for machine gun effect on "Bonnie & Clyde'," and an ocarina solo on the Bee Gee's "Holiday." In the summer of 1968, Snow, and Lopez left the band and Wilson and Arnold joined the military. At that point, Mike McRoberts answered an ad in the Peach Section of the local paper, auditioned, and joined. This version of the band included McRoberts on keyboard; Steve Downey, guitar; Mike Musick, bass; and Doug Lindsey on drums. McRoberts recalled that "we were popular and played gigs almost every weekend. Mostly we played high school dances and teen clubs. During the 1960s, the Jokers opened local performances for several stars including Sam the Sham and the Pharaohs, Gary Lewis and the Playboys, Daughters of Eve, the Blue Things, and the Flippers.

Sometime in the spring of 1969, Steve and Mike Musick left and the group auditioned for other musicians. They were about to give up, but as McRoberts remembered, "in June of 1969 we were offered a gig at Lancers East backing a singer, Betty McRae. We then added Greg Stevens on guitar and George Mueller on bass. I played organ and piano. We would do a set and then back Betty for a set." This arrangement lasted for just a short time, with members going on to join other bands. McRoberts, for example, first joined a very short-lived band called Clavius, followed by Syzygy. McRoberts then went on to a music career that included working for Akai to develop features, such as the MPC60.

Photos courtesy: Phil Snow

Courtesy: the Illusions

The Illusions

Formed in early '60s, the Illusions included Rod Haines; Larry Hughes; Larry Webster; Ron Starkel; Jim Young; Jim Mckay; Lindsey Cutsinger; Dave Ellis; Wade Williams. They got into playing the early psychedelic rock in the mid and later '60s. They competed in a Battle of The Bands at Wichita's Cotillion. They appeared at the Stage Door Inn, The Attic and The Workshop as well as numerous frat and barn parties around the state. They were a regular band at El Dorado's "The Cage".

Courtesy: Mark Archibald

Doug and the Inn-truders

This group's story started at Horace Mann Middle School. A group of friends came together to play music, practicing in the school gym. At first, it was just Doug Terbush on lead guitar and vocals, Art Martinez on rhythm guitar and Mike Jimenez on drums. Inspired by the music of Buddy Holly and Ritchie Valens, they played school dances, T.A.R.P. events, and even performed at the 54 drive in for the showing of the Beatles' film, A Hard Day's Night. Doug and the Inn-truders were a regular participant in the battle of the bands and recorded their instrumental hit, "What's Up" for the Wichita's Aircap Records. The band members just wanted to play music and sometimes had to be encouraged to get out and play more. Martinez recalled that Doug's mother was the group's "backbone." Terbush's mom had the car and passion for promotion, to make a number of events happen. Later on Mike Jimenez left the group and Greg Dunn replaced him on the drums.

By 1967, a new set of musicians came on board and had more of a horn band sound. Among them were Rick Meyer who later went on to play in the Breakers, and Bruce Simpson. Roger Walls played trumpet. Terbush himself was accomplished in both guitar and saxophone and even had an eye screw in his guitar so that he could easily hook his Fender onto the saxophone strap. Terbush continued as a musician, playing alongside Bryan Hill at the Camelot Club in the group Mini-Max.

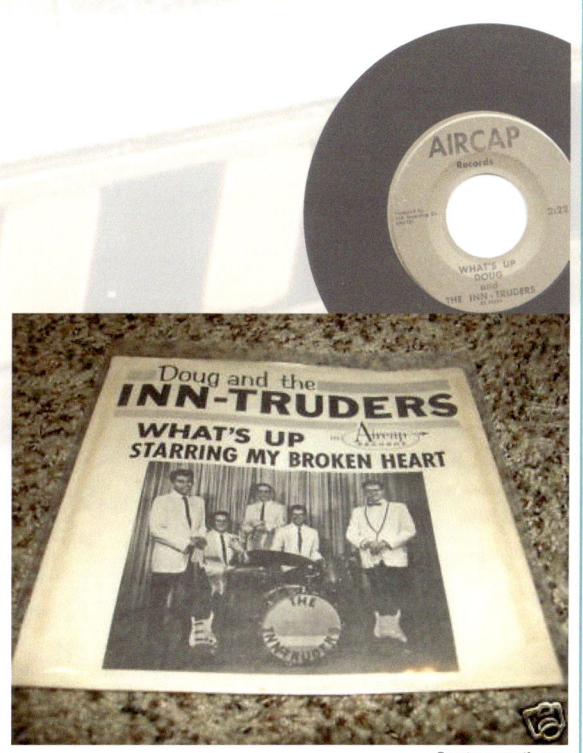
Courtesy popsike.com

Mr. Roberts and the Rhodesmen

Courtesy: the Rhodesmen

Formed about 1965 in Colorado Springs, the band's key members relocated to Wichita. It consisted of Doug Bailey, who also played with the Blue Banana; Ronnie 'Doc' Williams; Wayne Roberts; and drummer Danny Loveland. At first, the band performed at the Seneca Lounge but soon after, relocated to the Green Onion. The group even recorded an album called the "*Little Red Book*." It was at that point, however, that the group underwent some changes. Loveland left to go back to the Seneca Lounge and Jim Kincaid took his place. By the late 1960s, the band's members had gone on to new opportunities, most notably Wayne Roberts, who went on to play with the Soul Survivors.

Daniel and the Lions Den

Courtesy: the Lion's Den

From 1965 to 1966, this band included Danny Wilson on lead guitar and Bob Byrne on bass. They were regular features at clubs like the Red Dog Inn, and even opened for Booker T and the MG's, transporting their equipment in a black hearse.

The group broke up in 1967 when several band members were drafted and went to Vietnam. Their legacy lived on through some of the band members' classmates, like Dan Monnat, who came over to listen to practice sessions.

Photos courtesy: Phil Black

The Prophets

Formed in mid-1964 on the heels of the British Invasion, this quartet—Phil Black and Dave Rice, guitars; Doug Trowbridge, bass; and Jim "mouse" Beggs, drums—focused on tight harmonies and a repertoire that ran the gamut from the Mersey Beat to Motown.

The band was a local favorite performing at teen clubs such as Howards, the Attic and the Carrousel, as well as sock hops and high school dances around Kansas.

In late 1964, with the addition of Dell Cady on bass, the band opened for the Beach Boys at the Wichita Forum. When observed peering through a crack in the stage door following their performance, the band was besieged by adoring fans and forced to seek refuge backstage until the crowd dispersed. While members changed—Jim Kent; keyboards, Danny Personne, drums; and Mike Daniels, lead vocals—the group continued to perform the hit songs of the day.

In a display of unity, when a band member received his military draft notice in June of 1966, three members of the group decided to join the Marines Corp together. Tragically, singer Mike Daniels was killed in September of 1967 in Vietnam.

The Prophets covered a variety of material—The Beatles, James Brown and even a dose of Detroit Soul. With a focus on harmonies and tight arrangements, the band earned a strong following around the Wichita area.

Teen Clubs such as the Attic, Howard's and the Carrousel Club were favorite venues brimming with fans to hear this band.

The Twisters

Photos courtesy: Ed Curiel

One of the first rock & roll/rhythm & blues bands to come out of Reno County, the Twisters included Jewell Bernard, guitar; James Dawson, bass; Paul Hale, vocals & sax; Ed Curiel, drums; George Reeves, trumpet. Named after a brand of wine, the Twisters played nightclubs and other venues throughout the region. They were the first rock & roll band to perform at the Fox Theatre in Hutchinson.

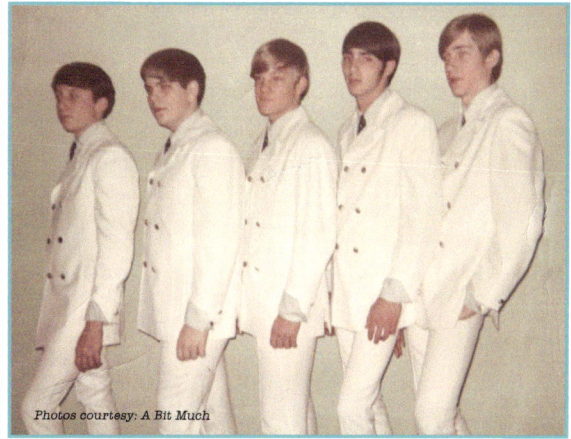
Photos courtesy: A Bit Much

A Bit Much

A group comprised of students from Kapaun High school was among three national winners in a contest sponsored by Jenkins Music, in conjunction with Vox, internationally known manufacturer of guitars, amps, and organs. Each Vox dealer held a contest and sent tapes of the winning three combos in their area to Vox headquarters for judging. The band was: Jim Doherty, Rudy Gans, Bob Kendrick, Vince Colling, and John Burnett.

Fifteen rock & roll bands took part in Wichita's contest at the Cotillion ballroom. The band won an all-expense-paid trip to Forest Hills, New York, to compete with the other two national winners. They placed second in the finals and received $2,500 worth of Vox equipment and sponsor Vox equipment for one year.

Mad Hatters

Courtesy: Mad Hatters

In 1964, a group of junior high school friends formed the Mad Hatters when they got to South High Jim Peterson was on lead guitars, Jay Bruff on keyboard, Bruce Sell on drums, Gary Watson on bass, and John Rogers on saxophone and bass, as well as Rick Gardner and Kenny Long on trumpet. Known for their horn playing, they performed at proms, local venues, and battles of bands. They later purchased a bus to tour across Kansas and Oklahoma, one of their most popular venues being the Lamplighter in Manhattan. It was good money for these teenagers, who certainly had a good time could not be too rowdy since the band's managers included Jay Bruff's parents, Jim and Jo. Jim Bruff was a Wichita policeman and Jo also worked for the police department! The Mad Hatters had ties to another south side horn band, the Bishops as John Rogers and Kenny Long were brothers of Bishops' members Jim Rogers and Earl Long. In 1970, Rogers left the Mad Hatters to continue his education and Rick Meyer became the new saxophonist. Soon after, Jay Bruff left to go to college and was replaced by Jay Leach. When that happened, the Mad Hatters transformed themselves into a new manifestation of the Apostles.

Pat McJimsey

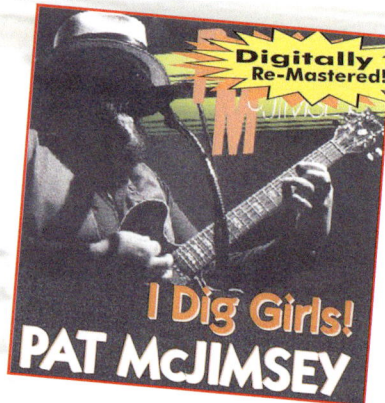

A double threat on guitar and vocals, Pat McJimsey fronted many bands throughout his career, beginning at the age of 17—Velvet Honey, Bear Valley Blues Band, the Entire British Navy, Patch, the KFDI Country Swing band and 4 Brothers.

Shortly before his death, McJimsey digitally remastered the *I Dig Girls* Album originally released in the '80s, and was planning a new all blues album.

Upon his death the Performers Assistance Trust (PAT) was established to offer financial help to musicians who can no longer perform due to major illness, accident or medical emergency or to their survivors to help with final expenses.

McJimsey was inducted into the Kansas Music Hall of Fame in 2011.

The Restless Knights

First called The Servants of September the group realized after a while that it wasn't a very "cool" name and didn't fit well on a bass drum! So they changed it. The new name was publicized in newspaper articles in the El Dorado Times and the Southeast High School paper. The group consisted of Rick Wilcoxson, lead singer; Robert White, lead guitar; Randy Barb, rhythm guitar; Tom Lemming, bass guitar; Rick Burrus, drums. They played at private parties and school dances around Wichita and at the Cotillion, and at the Cage in El Dorado.

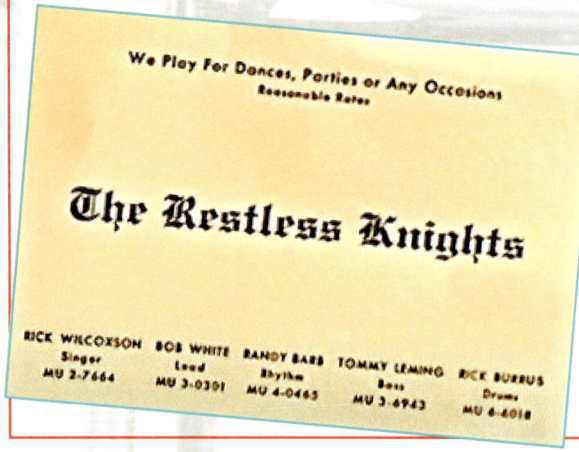

The Camelots

Courtesy: the Camelots

Playing from 1963 to 1964, the Camelots consisted of Ronnie Macklin and Jim Williams on guitar, Burt Tims on bass, Ken Bloomquist on drums, and Joe Villafane on keyboard. Bloomquist recalled "we played quite a lot at Dearmore's as well as at other local venues and parties. We were quite popular and played rock & roll of the day quite well." In 1964, the band broke up with Tims and Bloomquist going on to play with the Serfs.

Photos courtesy: Rodney & the Blazers

Rodney and the Blazers

In Coffeyville, Kansas, bassist Rodney Lay and drummer Bob York got to know each other by playing with a group known as the Off-Beats. In 1960, York and Lay teamed up with guitarist Pete "Peaches" Williams and saxophonist Bob "Sir Robert" Scott to form the group Rodney and the Blazers. They soon added keyboardist Don Downing, who joined Lay in lead vocals. A mixed race band, Rodney and the Blazers became a popular local group, playing Friday nights at the El Rancho Opera House between Coffeyville and Independence. The region southeast of Wichita had developed an impressive community of musicians and Williams had been taught by one of the area's best known figures, Leon "Crutch" Crutchfield.

Originally based in Coffeyville, Rodney and the Blazers soon went on the road, playing at the Seattle World's Fair, New York, Arizona, New Jersey, Philadelphia, Baltimore, and British Columbia. They became known for their distinctive look: they wore blazers instead of jackets (hence the group's name), colored their hair silver, and did something that was unusual for musicians back then: they wore sunglasses on stage. They began to record, releasing the single "Teenage Cinderella," on their Kampus label. In Philadelphia, Lay learned that one of the city's main disc jockeys predicted that he would be the next Elvis.

The band continued to tour and in 1961 even joined a six-week tour with Bill Haley & the Comets. When that tour ended in Mexico City, however, Williams, Scott, and Downing left the band. In the years that followed, Lay and York brought in a number of other musicians, including Gene Bongiorni, Chan Romero, Skip Knape, Sam Beck, Dennis Winton, and, for a time, Mary Taylor on vocals. The band continued to tour and even appeared on the television show Star Route in 1964 before breaking up in 1965.

Rudy Love

A staple in the music industry since the 1960s, Rudy Love has attained a status shared by few musicians. His career session work includes recording with such greats as Ray Charles, Stevie Wonder, Carlos Santana, Chaka Kahn, Barry White and Billy Preston to name just a few.

In the late 1960s, Love went on the road with rock & roll legend Little Richard. Eventually tiring of the fast pace of the road, Love returned to Wichita and with the assistance of his siblings helped form Rudy Love and the Love Family Band. While the act has taken on many different incarnations over the years, it remained a local favorite.

In the early 1970s, Love journeyed to Detroit and Motown Records where he worked as a demo vocalist and logged session work with Marvin Gaye as well as the Temptations.

By 1974 Love had joined one of the most popular acts of the era as musical director for Sly and the Family Stone, and for the next 10 years he toured around the world with this band.

Branching out into a solo career, his 1997 disc *Out of Rhythm* went platinum in Europe and Asia.

Love was inducted into the Kansas Music Hall of Fame in 2011.

Courtesy: Rudy Love

Lo & Behold

In 1967, a group of classmates at Truesdell Junior High formed Lo & Behold. The band consisted of Curt Poole on guitar; Bill Harrel on bass, and & Cliff Tipton on drums. The following year, Jerry Powell, who had previously worked with Cliff, joined to play the Hammond Organ. All the members sang, but Tipton and Powell were the primary vocalists.

This was the first band for Poole and Harrel, while Powell was already playing like the legendary Jimmy Smith. Tipton had started playing drums with his dad's band when he was around 6 years old. By the time the band formed, Tipton "knew how to play anything with strings on it," as Poole recalled.

Lo & Behold started playing at local skating rinks, and teen dances at local spots like Meadowlake Beach and by the summer of 1970, had become the house band at the Gasser club in south Wichita. The band broke up when Tipton's family moved out of state in 1971. Cliff Tipton eventually moved back to Wichita around 1974 and played in several other bands before moving to Nashville, playing with a country group called "The Montana Band." Powell went with the Velvet Rainbow while Harrel and Poole eventually became part of the Lost Souls.

Sinners Repent/Smokey Bear

In the late 1960s, some middle school friends formed a band called Sinners Repent that included Steve Swaim on drums, Ken Malner as lead guitar, and Bud Mitchner on bass, and later Bruce Stevens, and in 1968, Franz Johann (John) Corkum joined the band, initially to provide sound and lights, but later became the main vocalist. Later on, Mike Horton played rhythm guitar.

From 1968 through 1970, the group performed as Smokey Bear at Skateland, the teen club at McConnell Air Force Base, and various sock hops and at battles of the bands. Performing music like that of Hendrix and Creedence Clearwater Revival, the band even recorded an album at Hi Fidelity Studios. Corkum, in addition to vocals, ran sound and lights. Smokey Bear was one of the early bands in Wichita to include sound and light shows in their concerts. Towards the end of the band's time, guitarist David Fleming joined, recalling that occasionally, the band played under the name Mud Flap.

Tradewinds/Gold Plush Blues

The original Tradewinds were: Curtis Payne on guitar and vocals; Bobby Mitchell on lead vocals; Jim Quincy on bass; Larry Bally on drums; Ron Mueller on Cordavox (and on accordion with a Leslie speaker cabinet).

Known for its performances, the band wore matching outfits and did coordinated steps. They won one of the 1967 Uhlik happenings at the Cotillion against 19 other bands. The group played lots of church dances, armories, and teen clubs through 1968. Greg Stevens joined the group after Bobby Mitchell left as lead singer/guitarist and performed until fall of 1968. The Tradewinds regrouped as the Gold Plush Blues in 1969 without Ron and Greg.

Common Ground

From 1966 and 1967, Common Ground was known as a lightshow/psychedelic progressive rock band, playing Yardbirds, The Who, and Jimi Hendrix. The group consisted of Mike Olsen on the lead guitar, Jim Mullins on drums (who later became a jazz drummer in Detroit), and Hal Davis as the lead singer. The other band members included a guitarist named Lonnie, and a bassist named Michael. Along with Jim, they were from Hutchinson. They played venues in both towns. Their biggest claim to fame was leading off for The Kingsmen at the Cotillion ballroom.

Blue House

Formed in 1967 the Blue House performed traditional and hard rock blues in the local bar scene. Their first gig was at a bar outside of El Dorado. The main guitarist was Clif Major, who formed the band after the break up of the Outcasts, along with another legacy of the Outcasts, drummer Neal McGaugh. The band included guitarist Michael Olsen, and vocals by Hal Davis. As Davis recalled, "Blue House and the Outcasts had very similar repertoires so whether it was the Yardbirds or The Who or just standard blues/rock songs we didn't need to rehearse very much." A year after the band broke up, Mike Olsen was electrocuted while working with a construction crew in 1969.

The Bishops

They played many homecomings and proms in the Wichita area and a standing gig at the McConnell Air Force Base NCO club many Friday nights. They also got to play at Renfro's in Emporia; The Touch of Gold Club in Topeka; and in Atchison and Goodland.

They were Earl Long, guitar; Jim Rogers, lead vocals; John Kenyon, Hammond B3; Steve House, sax; Brad Barrett, drums; Robin(Chris) Church, trumpet; George Naylor, trumpet; Richard Lamb, trombone and bass.

The first vehicle the band bought was an International Harvester mail truck. It only had one side door and a "garage" style door in the back and the side door didn't have a seal. On the trip to Goodland, one of the fathers drove them. They all gyped school on a Friday to travel to Goodland and it was an extremely cold day. Their gas line was freezing as they traveled up Broadway (US 81) to get to I-70.

They pulled into the Sedgwick County fire station at 53rd and Broadway, because the driving father was a cousin to the Captain there and a volunteer fireman as well. They allowed them to park inside the station for a while to let them and the truck thaw out, gave the band some gas-line antifreeze and they continued on. Since there was no seal on the door, they bought a roll of duct tape and every time they stopped for gas (which was frequently), after everyone was inside, they taped up the door to keep the cold out. Of course there was only one seat for the driver and no seat belts. Somehow they survived with 9 people and all their equipment, which included a Hammond B3, two Leslies, two Voice of the Theatre speakers, light boxes, amps, instruments and the show clothes and luggage. As it turned out, they just played the gig for the PR because they spent every dime they made and then some for the motel room and food in Goodland that night.

Family Circle

A short-lived band, the Family Circle included Steve Downey, guitar and lead vocal; Dick Parsley, organ and lead vocal; Terry Hacker, bass guitar; Thane Rogers, drums; Richard Lamb, trombone; Steve House, sax and flute; and Robin "Chris" Church on trumpet. They were crazy about Chicago and did lots of their tunes. They played at a few clubs in town including Dearmores. They only lasted four months but had a little magic to it and shot a very cool promo pic. Regarding the band's end, one member recalled simply "I think other opportunities just came up for some of us."

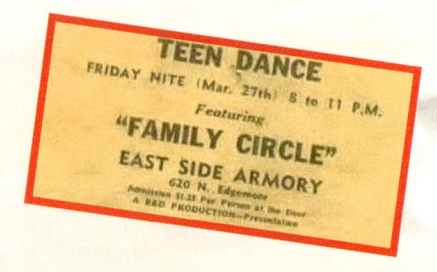

Velvet Rainbow/Boogie

Courtesy: Terrry Hacker

In 1969, Billy Wullschleger had come back to Wichita, forming a duo with Randy Rickman that played at a little bar called the Coach Light. It became the basis of a group initially called The Velvet Rainbow and included Randy Rickman, lead vocals & guitar; Jerry Powell, organ; Jack Howard, bass; and Billy Wullschleger on drums. Later on, Jack Howard left the band and they brought in Bob Anthony for the bass. Later on, the band added Billy Harrel on bass. This group broke up but eventually several band members including Powell, Wullschleger and Rickman came together to form Boogie.

Boogie started in the early 1970s with Bill Wullschleger on drums, Lance Threet on lead guitar, Perry Overstake on bass, Spencer Sutton on the Hammond organ, and a lead vocalist the band remembers only as Scott. They started out playing at the Chesterfield Club by WSU. Later on, Boogie had Bobby Mitchell on vocals and Mike Andrews on the Hammond, Perry Overstake on bass, LD Mingle on guitar, and Bill Wullschleger on drums. The band then changed when part of the old Velvet Rainbow members coming in including Randy Rickman and Jerry Powell. Later on, Larry Mingle joined the band, with Terry Hacker on bass and Norman Mehl on keys. Then the band morphed with Gary Heitz on guitar. The last version of Boogie was Curt Poole, Billy Harrel, Mehl, and Wullschleger. Boogie had the honor of being the opening act for some well-known national groups including Ted Nugent, The Continental Kids. Throughout, Boogie was a mix of top 40 and progressive rock. By then, they played a number of clubs in Wichita like the Casino, Stage Door Inn, The New Image, Central Station, Scene '70s as well as road gigs like the Lamplighter and Red Pussycat in Salina, Dark Horse and Warehouse in Dodge City, and Eleanor Rigby's in Great Bend. By 1974, Boogie had broken up when Bill Harrel left the group, and the three remaining members joined with the horn section of Star, along with bassist Terry Hacker.

Courtesy: Harry Dobbin

Streetmasse

This band began as a replacement for "The Love Bugs" when Danny Loveland left the Penthouse Club. The pop sensibilities of the music there were changing with the advent of heavier and psychedelic influences.

It consisted of Steve McCaskey, bass; Harry Dobbin, guitar; Richard Hackley, keyboards; and Greg Feese, drums. They later played at a number of 3.2 bars – the Cedars, the Flicker and the King Cole Inn to name a few. The group later did change with the addition of Ken Bell on bass and Bill Hooper on guitar,

Photos courtesy: Jim Wood

Soule Survivors

The story of the Soule Survivors began with a group of friends in the mid-1960s who formed the band the Destinations. About 1967, the Destinations broke up and several of the musicians came together to form the Soul Survivors. The initial line up consisted of Baptiste "Bat" Shunatona on guitar, Mike Redd on bass, Gary Bussart on keyboard, and Don "Squeak" Cleary on drums. A short time later, Robin Ragland on vocals, Mike Ehrke on guitar, and Tom Golucci on saxophone

were added. At this point, the band added the "E" to soule. Known by some as "the best cover band that ever came about," the Soule Survivors initially played at Dearmore's.

The late 1960s offered new opportunities and several changes in the band line up. After playing for about two years at Dearmore's, the band shifted to playing at the Hi Ho. Meanwhile Cleary left to play with Finnigan and Wood, replaced by Jim Wood. Shunatona and Redd also left with Wayne Roberts from Mr. Roberts and the Rhodesmen joining them.

Afterwards, the group won a Battle of the Bands and became, in effect, the house band for the new Century II Civic Center. For a year, the Soule Survivors represented Century II and opened for a number of the major acts such as Helen Reddy.

The time at the Hi Ho lasted about two years as well when the owner of the club announced that he wanted to have a new, fresh band play so the Soule Survivors had to find a new home. For a time they played at the Fireside East and Fireside West. When Gary Beard formed a new club, Sound Sircus, the Soule Survivors became the house band for that venue. The group also did some touring and played at Mr. Lucky in Denver. Lasting until the Sound Sircus closed, the Soule Survivors inspired a whole new generation of younger musicians who formed the next wave of bands.

Courtesy: Cambridge Experiment

The Cambridge Experiment

In 1969, Joe Sauer, Ron Schauf, and Brad Bartlett began playing at local church and school events. With Mike Wurth, rhythm guitar and John Wurth, bass, they performed at the Mount Carmel Academy Talent Show in March of 1969 as " Top Banana and the Rest of the Bunch– the Sound with Appeal." Later in 1969, they formed the Cambridge Experiment with Joe Sauer, lead guitar and vocals; Ron Schauf, rhythm guitar and vocals; Brad Bartlett, drums; and Jeff Harms, bass and vocals. The band's second phase began in 1970 with Joe Sauer, lead guitar and vocals; Ron Schauf, bass, guitar and vocals; Brad Bartlett, drums; and Tim Malone, piano, organ, guitar, vocals and bass. Again, playing youth events, swimming pools were especially common locations for their gigs. The band performed until 1971 when Malone left to go to school.

The Lost Souls

Courtesy: the Lost Souls

The Lost Souls formed in 1967. The original members were all from Carlton Junior High, south of Wichita and included Clyde Tarrance, vocals and showman extraordinaire; Bob McFarland, guitar and vocals; Bryan Forrester, bass guitar and vocals, and Randy Holden, drums.

The band started by rehearsing at their friend, Debbie Avenell's barn, which was on the property of D&M Hardware on K-15 just south of Wichita. As with most young bands, The Lost Souls started by playing a few gigs at places like Skateland South, The Teen Bunny Club, The Teen Club at McConnell AFB, and school dances, but the band also began getting booked into nightclubs like The Gasser Club and Lancer's East. Clyde had an amazing talent for capturing the crowd with his singing, but more so with his dancing. Clyde could dance like James Brown; with turns, twists and jumping off the stage into the splits. The nightclub crowds would go crazy over this floor show, so the band was asked back many times. Of course, they were far too young to be in nightclubs, so Bryan's mom, Ellen "Mama June" Forrester, took over as manager/chaperone.

The Lost Souls went through a few member changes along the way. Doug Lindsey (from the Jokers) took a short stint on the drums, but eventually, Rusty Cherry settled in keeping the beat. Gus Meeuwen joined the band on lead guitar around 1969. Curt Poole on guitar and Rodney Lovett on organ joined about the same time in late 1970. Bill Harrel on bass and Lloyd Miller on drums replaced Forrester and Cherry when they left to form Standard American. After a few months, however, Bill Harrel left to join Velvet Rainbow. Miller & Poole stayed on with the Lost Souls for a time but wanted to play a different style of music and eventually left the Lost Souls to form "Sunset" with Bill Harrel.

Courtesy: Phil Black

Magpie

In the early to mid 1970s, Wichita native Phil Black returned from California with two band mates—David Roush and John Grosse. The band brought with them a wealth of original material, close harmonies and tight arrangements. The band included John Grosse, bass and vocals; Phil Black, guitar and vocals; and David Roush, guitar and vocals. Magpie soon added drummer Johnny Dondlinger to round out the group, and for several years the band played around the Wichita area to the delight of their many fans.

In 1972, the band moved to Memphis, TN, seeking recording opportunities. The band reunited in Memphis for a concert in 2015.

Hard Road

Formed in 1969, Hard Road went through several versions. With bassist Jerry Cusick as a founding member and key performer throughout the band's various incarnations, Hard Road's first version also included  John Bonner on guitar, Don Overstake on keyboard, Gary Wallace and Mike Willcut on drums, and Richard Walters on keyboard. All did vocals while female vocalist Connie White provided a Janis Joplin sound.

A year later, the band changed with Cusick and Overstake remaining and adding Ralph Leite, Russ Weise, Brad Bartlett on  drums and Ron Russ on guitar. Vocals came from Russ and Overstake with Connie White, C.C. Neal and Bobby Mitchell.

By 1975, the band changed again with Jerry Powell on keyboards, Pat Preboth on drums, Cusick on bass, and vocals coming from Powell, Preboth, Mickey Estes, Randy Rickman, and C.C. Neal.

Hard Road was a top 40 soul band that played at clubs including Lancers East, which became The White House. It was also the house band at the Camelot Club and the Chesterfield Club. Hard Road toured nationally working with Dick Clark Productions and the ABC Booking agency. The group was able to do a number of tours, culminating in an extended tour to Texas, Arizona, and California. The band lasted until 1976.

Photos courtesy: John Bonner

Open Mind

About 1970, a group of high school friends came together to form the band Open Mind. Line up included guitarist David Fleming, who had previously been playing with Smokey Bear, Bud Mitchner on bass, and Woody Schrader on drums. For a short time, Lance Threet and Kevin Jones practiced with the group, but did not perform with them. Although the group's members were young, they were able to play a lot of prominent events, including for Governor Docking, the Junior Chamber of Commerce, and the Petroleum Club. Once called "one of the Top Ten bands in Wichita," Open Mind owed a lot of its success to its promoter, Ed Trautwein, who band members simply knew as "Ratty." He kept the band at a grueling touring schedule, even having them play in far western Kansas over a weekend with the members hurrying back to make it to school for the week. Open Mind continued to play until the mid 1970s, when the various members went to join other groups.

The Brotherhood

Formed about 1968, The Brotherhood was made up of East High students who played mostly school dances, several company parties, and at the clubs at McConnell AFB such as the Officers Club, NCO Club, Servicemen's Club. The lineup included Jon Weaver, lead guitar; Jim Beebe, drums; Gene Turner, bass; and Rob Henline, rhythm guitar. In addition to their club and dance gigs, The Brotherhood also participated in "Battle Of The Bands" at the Cotillion Ballroom. By 1972, the group disbanded when Turner and Henline joined the U.S. Air National Guard.

Mama's Pride and Syzygy

In the 1960s, a short-lived group called Mama's Pride formed with John Frederickson on vocals, Charlie Darling on guitar, Larry Snow on guitar, Woody Reed on drums, Ira Pray on bass, and Jay Jones on keyboards.

In 1967, Frederickson and Darling formed a new group, Syzygy, with Rick Hodge on bass; Kathy Ring Miller on vocals; Ron Black on congas; Mike McRoberts on keyboards; and Amboo Ploy on drums. Kenny Morrison added percussion duties a bit later, as did violinist, Nancy Buchen.

They started in with clubs, battle of the bands, proms, parties, and whatever gigs they could find. They did lots of demo work in Hi-Fidelity Studios. Kathy was well known as a singer according to Hodge, "if you shut your eyes, you would think you were listening to Janis Joplin." Frederickson was a performer in his own right, more than once flailing the tambourine so hard until he broke a wrist.

By the early 1970s, Frederickson went on to become a DJ, "Little John." McRoberts went to play with the Jokers and Tin Ear. Hodge went to perform with Crank. After time in California, Ploy went to play with The Weasels. Black went on to a successful career in LA.

Heavy

For the North High Junior Assembly in February 1969, a group of students formed a band they called "Heavy," a name culled from Iron Butterfly's debut album. The band featured Greg "Fingers" Taylor on organ; Kip Ehrke, guitar; Bill Powell, drums; and Dave Shaw on Bass. Kip Ehrke continued to pursue music and Taylor played harmonica with Larry Raspberry and the Highsteppers as well as being a founding member of Jimmy Buffett's Coral Reefer Band.

The Livin' End

Shortly after the British Invasion, a group of North High School and John Marshall Junior High kids got together to play the music of the Beatles, Stones and the Animals. The band, was comprised of Jim Walker, guitar; Kip Ehrke, guitar; Roger Milller, bass; Bob Spencer, organ and harmonica; Dan Wulz, drums; and Sam Dennis, vocals.

Chaparrals / Solomon and the Monarchs

Formed in 1964, and made up of high school students from Southeast, the Chaparrals consisted of David Maib on rhythm guitar/vocals; Jeff Towner on bass guitar; Tim Grove on drums; and Mike Olson on lead guitar and vocals. The following year, the band evolved into Solomon and the Monarchs and added Harold Davis as lead singer. Playing sock hops and other venues, they played the Beatles, Rolling Stones, Beach boys, Chuck Berry and popular British groups like Hermans Hermits. The main band members consisted of Mike "Mo" Olsen, lead guitar; Jeff Towner, bass; Harold Davis, lead singer; Tim Grove on drums and David Maib, rhythm guitar/vocals. They won the first KLEO/HIS Battle of the bands at the Cotillion, for which they got a $500 gift certificate from HIS clothing. After that, they got a manager and were booked most weekends for the next year before they broke up over "creative music differences." Davis and Olsen continued on to perform together in Common Ground and Blue House.

Patch

Hired by a group of teenagers to provide sound equipment for their first gig—a Saturday 7:30 a.m. Walk for Mankind—inside Henry Levitt Arena, Kenny Potter heard a band of young kids pounding out some pretty solid rock and roll.

Photos courtesy: Jim Hill

Between sets, Potter approached the band to give them some positive feedback. The group needed a singer and a PA and Potter needed a band. In short order, a new group was formed—Jimmy Hill, guitar; Chris Hutchens, guitar; Craig Neitfeld, bass; David Pence, drums and Kenny Potter, vocals. With the slapdash fashion the group was put together Patch seemed a perfect name.

The group's age was such a concern, that Potter, the dutiful elder statesmen of the group, actually carried handwritten waivers signed by each of the musician's parents. This method of parental consent may seem strange by today's standards, but it's important to remember that these were more innocent times and this was not that uncommon as a practice in that era. Potter is quick to add that while the group was often underage for the venues they played, the band members were always professional and respectful and no one ever questioned their presence.

For out-of-town weekend gigs, Potter would pick up the band in front of East High in a yellow and blue Rainbow Bread truck purchased from a member of his former band, Spare Change. Soon, they were playing around Wichita in taverns, nightclubs and at raves as well as many out of town engagements.

In 1972, an unexpected call from local blues guitarist Pat McJimsey inquiring if they needed an additional guitarist and singer. Without hesitation, McJimsey was added to the roster. The band decided to also add Alan Baugh on Hammond B-3. In 1975, three band members left the band; however, Jim Hill, Dave Pence and Craig Neitfeld continued with the addition of guitarist Kent Havener. The band continued to perform around the area until 1977.

Lander Ballard

Ballard began playing guitar when he was 6 years old, starting a band when he was 13 and played through high school. He joined the Air Force and went to Vietnam, and played in a GI show band for all service branches.

Courtesy: Lander Ballard

Moving to Wichita in 1970, he began his solo career, playing rock, pop, blues and R&B. He has played every kind of venue you can imagine - bars, clubs, concerts and colleges.

Ballard travelled to Nashville to record and learn the trade - starting his own record label and publishing company. In 1977 he released his first LP, *High Time* and the single "My Friends" got air time around the South and Midwest.

He has been the featured act at many concerts and shows, and has opened for many acts, including Rory Gallagher, Stephen Stills, Bonnie Raitt, John Hartford, Leon Russell, Shawn Phillips, America, Roger McGuinn, Chris Hillman and more.

Besides his performance skills, Lander has been known for breaking guitar strings. Without stopping when one breaks, he continues to sing a capella, changes the string, tunes it, and picks up wherever he is in the song.

The Continentals

Courtesy: Dwain Terry

Forming in the late 1960s, the Continentals consisted of Jan Smith, bass; Dwain Terry, guitar; and Doug Thomas, lead guitar. Their drummer was Tom Wise, the younger brother of Bob and Don Wise of the Rock-N-Tones. Playing Carl Perkins tunes along with some early 1960s rock and county, the group performed local clubs as well as with Ray Sawyer of Dr. Hook and the Medicine Show. In 1972, they even recorded at a small studio in Wichita but the quality was so poor that Terry remembered "it sounded like everything was in a puddle."

Jerry Hahn Brotherhood

Courtesy: Jerry Hahn Brotherhood

A musician who crossed the boundaries of rock, jazz, blues, and country with remarkable ease, Jerry Hahn learned to play guitar at the Wiley Guitar Store and showed such promise that he started appearing on television with Bob Wiley when they were kids. After studying at Wichita State University, Hahn moved to San Francisco, playing with John Handy, The 5th Dimension, and Gary Burton. In 1970, he formed his own group, Jerry Hahn Brotherhood, consisting of Hahn on guitar, banjo, and vocals; Mike Finnigan on piano, organ, harmonica, and vocals, Clyde Graves on bass, and George Marsh on drums. The band produced one album in 1970 which included the song "Captain Bobby Stout", a song written by Lane Tietgen named for a well known Wichita police officer. The song was later recorded by Manford Mann's Earth Band. The brotherhood was short-lived, with Mike Finnigan going on to team up with Jerry Wood. In 1973 Hahn and Marsh recorded a new album, *Fantasy*. In 1975, Hahn formed the more jazz/soul/funk oriented group, Jerry Hahn and his Quintet. Hahn continued his teaching career at Wichita State University through the 1980s, continuing to develop his techniques for playing jazz guitar. His book, *Jerry Hahn Method For Jazz Guitar*, came out in 2003.

Donny Overstake/Lotus

Originally from Winfield, Donny Overstake founded his first band while a student at Wichita State University. This was the first of a series of informal student groups that included The Hoi Poloi and Ginger Blue. Overstake then left to serve in Vietnam.

He returned to Wichita in 1970, getting a call from John Bonner inviting him to play for Hard Road at the Colony Club. By 1972, he had left that band and got together with some musicians from the WSU days, forming a band to play the Fireside. The band's original name was Crow Haven Farm, but soon, Overstake renamed it Lotus after a band he had heard in Australia. Lotus played at the Fireside and Scene '70s among others, before going on tour under American Bands Management. In Killeen, Texas, playing a club where people ate while listening to music. This was a far cry from Wichita, where locals were unaccustomed to eating in the same room with live music.

Then the group returned to Wichita in 1974, playing at Scene '70s. The scheduling was grueling, performing six nights a week past 2 a.m., and the exhausted musicians drifted apart. At that point, Pat Preboth approached Overstake about reconstituting Lotus. With Mickey Estes on guitar, Overstake on keyboard and vocals, and Don Keys on bass/keyboard, the group got an invitation from Dan Daniels, owner of the Fireside Club to perform. The trio had no bass player and Don began playing bass lines utilizing a key bass with his left hand.

The group struggled. At one time Overstake's friend, Pat McJimsey, came in and point blank asked Donnie "do you have any idea what you are doing?" Things changed when a young African American radiologist named John Smith started singing and Lotus took off.

Overstake bought the Fireside in 1975 and the business owner side dictated different musical decisions from his playing with Lotus. By 1985 with John Smith in declining health and Randy Rickman came in, bringing an era-correct "hair band" feel to the group. At the club, however, crowds demanded dance music, top 40, and the omni present disco influence. Overstake also had to navigate Kansas' complicated liquor laws that required clubs to have membership but at least this got him to know his "members" on a personal basis.

In 1985, Overstake relocated the Fireside from Harry and Woodlawn to a new site on south Rock Road. Meanwhile, John Smith retired from the band and a new group of female singers came on board. Among them was young Martina Schiff, who performed with Lotus before going to Nashville and becoming a country star under her married name, Martina McBride. Meanwhile, bassist Bill Landrum, which brought an added vocal presence, joined the group.

In the 1990s, Overstake bought into a club on Douglas called the Safari, which hosted bands like Live Wire and Haze, among others. In 1992, Safari closed and Overstake remade the place into a Mexican restaurant/bar called Margarita's.

He had remembered that club in Texas that offered both food and entertainment and Margarita's was one of the early venues in Wichita to offer that mix as well. Lotus has continued to perform, both at Margarita's and across the city, adding and reinventing the band through new players. In 2004, for example, Lotus played at the Cotillion featuring Pat McJimsey, just months before McJimsey's death. Pat agreed to work with Lotus regularly and passed away before it could happen. Margarita's has continued to hosts bands such as the FunTones, Annie-Up, Lucky People and other music acts when Lotus is hired out or takes time off.

Photos courtesy: Donny Overstake

Redneck

While many bands in the 1960s favored outlandish names—Strawberry Alarm Clock, Iron Butterfly, Vanilla Fudge—one Wichita group summed up in a single word the antithesis of the flower power culture—Redneck.

The band was comprised of two members of the short-lived band Cottonwood—guitarist Bat Shunatona and bassist George Graybill—combined with vocalist Scott "Skeeter" Van Norstrand, guitarist Rick Azim and drummer Jim Dourghty.

The band first formed in the spring of 1969 and by late summer they were the house band, playing six nights a week at the Phone Booth, located in an old post office building near Harry and Edgemoor.

The steady rhythms provided by Graybill and Shunatona allowed guitarist Azim to solo freely, which led to many inspired jazz/rock improvisations. Often, powerhouse vocalist Van Nordstrand would join in on flute or congas. On most nights the club was crowded and much of the audience reclined on pillows in the back of the room to listen.

Once, when the band was having a particularly good night, Black Sabbath's lead guitarist Tony Iommi came to the club after a concert. So impressed with Redneck's set, he gave the band Atlantic Records founder and president Ahmet Ertegun's private phone number. Iommi said he would tell Ertegun to expect a call. The band's hopes for fame, however, were quickly dashed when after the gig they tried in vain to produce the business card, each band member hopelessly searching pockets and wallets for the missing number. It was never found.

In March of 1971, Azim and Dourghty left the band and the remaining members headed for Denver with high hopes and a demo tape. Unannounced, they walked into the office of Barry Fey, manager of Sugar Loaf and Zepher. He liked the tape and put them to work with David Keel now on drums.

The band returned to Wichita and the Phone Booth later that year with the addition of John Burnett on guitar. The band played around Kansas as well as various Sunday afternoon gigs in Riverside Park. In the spring of 1972 the band played its last gig.

The Ricochets

Formed in the early 1960s, this band of students at Marshall Middle School consisted of David Carie on guitar, Jay "J.D." Schwien on bass, Greg Harris on organ, Gary Hunt as lead singer, and Jim Kincaid on drums. When Kincaid left to join the Vibrations, the Ricochets had a number of other drummers including Bob Mansfield.

Inspired by the music of the Ventures, the band played at sock hops and local talent shows through the early 1960s. After the Beatles hit, the various band members went their ways. David was the best known of a musical set of siblings, even teaching at Starkey Music. During the summer of 1969, Carie, with Ron Hill and Debbie Allen, went on to form the group The Ragamuffins and played gigs in Colorado. Coming back to Wichita, Carie continued as an in-demand guitarist. It was during the Wichita Jazz Festival that David became friends with a young guitarist by the name of Pat Metheny. Inspired by musicians from rock to jazz to country, Carie remained an active figure in the local music scene until his death in 1979.

Photos courtesy: Harry Dobbin

Dove / Salty Oats

This band consisted of Ken Bell, bass; Harry Dobbin, guitar & vocals; Greg Feese, drums; and Jackie Keimig, guitar.

Starting out in mostly 3.2 bars in town, the band joined the Way Ministry and ended up touring from Ohio to Utah. They moved to Denver in 1970 to start a fellowship there. Every year they went to play a Way festival, "the Rock of Ages," in Ohio and recorded some original songs on the Almond Tree label, both singles and LPs. The band played often in Vail and Denver, and travelled much, including home to DooDah every year. Later, the band added Larry Bally on drums and Richard Hackley on keyboards.

White River

Photos courtesy: Fred Bonner

By the early 1970s, drummer Fred Bonner had already established himself in groups such as Dennis Hunt and the Hunters, Tiny Lyman and the Jukes, and the Inn Keepers. In 1973, he was a key figure in the formation of a new group, White River, consisting of himself on drums, Connie White on vocals; Jim McElroy on keyboards and some guitar; Steve Campbell on bass; and Gippy Ponder on guitar. While still forming, the group gained the attention of ABC booking who encouraged the band to go on the road.

Bonner recalled that other than for rehearsals, White River "never played Wichita ever." They were a traveling show band, complete with sound and light equipment. "Tuxedoes were required." They played their first gig on February 12, 1973, at a Holiday Inn in Little Rock, Arkansas. For the next two years, White River traveled to clubs from Texas to New York. One of their longest stints was in Memphis, Tennessee, where they played at the Why Not Lounge and other places where music icons like Elvis Presley and Buddy Miles were known to have been in the audience.

ABC treated the band well, providing decent wages, good accommodations, regular food and beverages, and even roses for the female band members. The band played well together and Bonner recalled it being like one big family that traveled from place to place in a convoy that carried the band and all the equipment.

The down side of the arrangement was the grueling schedule that required playing six nights a week. There was no time off, even for family emergencies and after about two years, the band members were starting to burn out. After a time, the band had changed, with members from other cities replacing members in what had started as an all-Wichita line up. In time, only Connie White and Fred Bonner remained of the original band. At times, new members included Ernie Oritz from Garden City on organ; San Antonio native Richard Noriega, Jr. on guitar; Luis Cusido, from Barcelona Spain on keyboards; and Dave Parker was on bass. The big change for the band was when White left the group in Memphis, replaced by Roxanne Bell from Dallas. By 1975, Bonner decided to return to Wichita as well and White River wound down soon after.

Courtesy Ron Starkel

Albatross

Albatross featured Ron Starkel, guitar; Bill Rhyne, bass; Perry Pittman, vocals; and Mike Wilber, drums. Albatross came together in 1970 from the survivors of a previous band of high school students in El Dorado. Starkel had recently left the Illusions. They decided to change the band name for a fresh start and chose "Albatross" after the old Fleetwood Mac tune (although they never played that song). As three of the four members of the band were still in high school, they did not play bars frequently, relying more on high school proms - Udall, Peabody, Tonganoxie, Leon and others and places like teen centers or the Nomar Theater in Wichita. Pittman dropped out, after a few months, due to parental guidance to concentrate on high school classes and sports. The group continued as a three piece and with Starkel on vocals. The band folded due to life changes that normally happen to youths of that age with jobs, families, and college taking priority.

Public Secret/Boulder

Photos courtesy: Jim Meyer

Formed in 1966, Public Secret was originally a three piece band and consisted of John Jackson, lead guitar, Gary Hopper on bass, and Gary Toothaker (followed by Jim Meyer) on drums. Later on, the group added Kelly Gilbert on vocals and flute and Pete Krehbiel or 'Rabbit" on the Hammond B-3. The group was to have opened for Jimi Hendrix at WSU but the opportunity vanished when Hendrix canceled that concert.

In 1970, the band changed its name to Boulder, just before gaining guitarist Jamey Ratzlaff. When Meyer left in 1971, the group went through a series of drummers. They were called the local "Santana Band" or the "Hendrix/Cream Band," but early on, they did originals, too. A few of their own songs were "Over My Shoulder", "Backwoods Country Girl", "Resurrection Pictures" and "Sweet Cocaine."

Courtesy: Standard American

Standard American

Formed in 1970, Standard American played at The Scene '70s night club for 3 1/2 years and had a large following. One advertisement from 1971 noted that the band was a "well rounded" group of performers that included Bryan Forrester on bass, Mike Kilpatric on lead guitar, Fred LaMaster on keyboards, Russ Cherry on drums, Bob McFarland on lead vocals, and Ron Black congas and vocals. The group was a rock cover band that played all the hits, plus some deeper cuts from bands like Deep Purple, ZZ Top, Bad Company, Santana, Three Dog Night, and The Guess Who. The same advertisement noted that the group played from 7 p.m. to 3 a.m. Wednesday through Saturday. The band lasted until 1973.

The New Destination

The journey for The New Destination began in the mid-60s, as five high school friends joined their talents in the basement of one of the members' homes. The group soon had several sets of songs worked out and began playing for private parties, local school proms, and colleges throughout the state, as well as the ever present battle of the bands.

The band performed at the Cotillion and other venues in the area and opened for national acts such as Bachman-Turner Overdrive, Rare Earth, Paul Revere and The Raiders, Ray Charles and Johnny Rivers. The group gained popularity throughout Kansas and Oklahoma and in the early '70s were playing the club circuit throughout the Midwest. After spending time on the road the group decided to settle back in Wichita and became the house band first at The Draft Board, then Dearmores and finally the Casino Club.

The original members were Mike Crabtree, Ronnie Grider, Randy Rickman, Bill Wullshleger, and Mike Debacher.

In late 1971 early 1972 the group decided to open their own club called The Central Station. During the same time, Crabtree, Childress, and another partner bought Meadow Lake Resort in South Wichita and the group performed there regularly as did many other local groups. As disco became the rage live music began to suffer and the group sold the club and went on to perform for awhile at the Scene '70s Club before finally disbanding in late 1976.

Photos courtesy: Mike Crabtree
Photo by Gary Buehler

above: 1970 Penthouse Club - Mike Hilton; Wayne Avery; Chuck Swartzlander; Mike Crabtree; Mike Keitle; Ira Pray.
Other members: Randy Spade, Robert Childress, and Wayne Roberts, Steve Downey.

below: top L to R: Robert Childress, lead guitar; Randy Spade, drums; bottom: Mike Crabtree, lead vocals; Winston Blair, bass; Chuck Swartzlander, keyboards

new destination

Real People, New Elements, Akteelew, and Cartunes

In 1971, guitarist Jerry Chadic was playing with bass player Stan Reynolds at the Candle Club with an electric drum machine they nicknamed "Leroy." Patrons did not know what to make of a band with no person doing the drumming so the group that formed called themselves "Real People" to confirm that there were actual human beings doing the performance. Performing at clubs like the Hi Ho and the Loser Club, Real People included Chadic on guitar and vocals, Reynolds on bass, and a number of real drummers including Kenneth Herman and later, Doug Byers. The group played "the 1950s and 1960s in the 1970s" but found itself playing a wide range of music. One time, KFDI asked the band to play in a country music battle of the bands and Real People came in third!

By 1976, the various band members had moved on and Chadic went on to form the band New Elements in El Dorado that included Chadic, Reynolds, Byers, and keyboardist Greg Smith. A while later, Chadic formed a band with several family members called Akteelew, the name a reverse of the name of Chadic's boyhood town in Oklahoma. Playing in Kansas and Oklahoma Akteelew consisted of Jerry Chadic, his brothers Stanley and Gary, sister Mira, Gayle Childs, Merry Merritt, and Chassis Craford. In more recent years, Chadic put together the band Cartunes that includes himself, drummer David Barton, singer Jo Ann Jenkins, keyboardist Cathy Mae, and locally prominent blues bassist Val Williams. The Cartunes are a regular feature for events such as the KEYN concert series.

Board Of Regents

Starting in the mid 1960s, the Board of Regents was the house band for the Stage Door Inn. Gary Hamlin was the guitar player and part owner of the Stage Door Inn, a former movie theater as Steve Downey recalled, "a big, funky-smelling place that catered to the 18 and up college crowd."

In the early days of the Inn, the Serfs were the main band playing there. Later on, however, Hamlin helped found the Board of Regents that replaced the Serfs as the band. Catering to the college crowd, the group was known for being a party band. By 1967 the group consisted of: Gary Hamlin, lead guitar; Rich Hutton, bass; Greg Trippel vocalist; Archie Eutsler, organ; Larry Campbell, drummer; Bert Canova, saxophone; and Ron Hamilton, trumpet.

The band played various places including Fireside West and were featured as the KEYN special party band, booked by disk jockey Dave Ryley until the end of 1968 when they became the house band at the Stage Door. Over the next year the band added new members.

In 1969, a live recording at the Stage Door Inn included: Ron Hamilton, trumpet & vocals; Bert Canova, tenor sax; Greg Trippel, lead vocals; Dave Sproul, trumpet and fluegelhorn; Archie Eutsler, Hammond organ; J.D. Schwien, bass; Jim Kincaid, drums; Gary Hamlin, guitar; Roger Lewis, trumpet and Fluegelhorn. The band recorded the following songs which it had played on a consistent basis while at the Stage Door Inn: "It's Not Unusual," "Classical Gas," "Beginnings," "Can't Turn you Loose," "A Little Help From My Friends," "Sitting in Circles," "Just One More Smile," "I Don't Want To Cry," and "Harlem Shuffle."

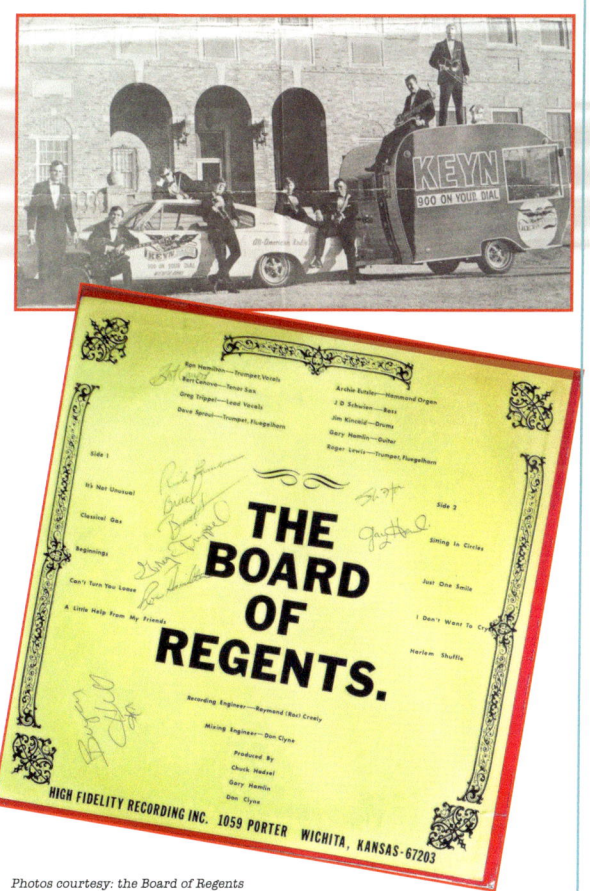

Photos courtesy: the Board of Regents

Courtesy: Spare Change

Spare Change

Kenny Dool on drums; Dick Reese on bass; Kenny Potter on vocals; Doug Webb on guitar; Charlie Collins on guitar; later Joe Martinez, guitar and Vic Peroo, manager - not pictured. The group took their name from the number of young panhandlers crowding street corners and concert sites of the late '60s and early '70s. The group formed in 1970 and were heavily influenced by English pop/blues acts such as Savoy Brown, Humble Pie, and Spooky Tooth. For several years the band performed at Wichita nightspots, Sunday afternoon Riverside Park concerts, as well as playing clubs around the state. At Wichita's Century II the group opened for the Dallas-based rockers Baby and Denver-based headliner SugarLoaf, who were riding the wave of a No. 1 hit single entitled *Green-Eyed Lady*.

Shine

When Tim Malone left The Cambridge Experiment to go to school, the rest of the band put an ad out in the Peach Section of the local paper for a new member. Margaret Rembleske, who played flute, answered, and Shine was born. The band consisted of Joe Sauer, lead guitar and vocals; Ron Schauf, bass and vocals; Gale Gilbert; piano and vocals; Margaret Rembleske, flute, and Brad Bartlett on drums. The band continued Cambridge Experiment's tradition of high school and teen events but also grew to play the Wichita Country Club, the Elk's Club, and the McConnell Officer's Club. The group also started touring, playing gigs in Lawrence and Wellington, among others.

In 1972, Bobby Mitchell from Boogie joined as lead singer, launching a second phase with Joe Sauer, lead guitar and vocals; Brad Bartlett, drums; Ron Schauf, bass; Gale Gilbert; keyboard and vocals; Margaret Rembleske, flute. Calling themselves the "fastest upcoming male and female show group in the Midwest." Shine was a regular feature at the Camelot Club. This version of Shine lasted until 1973. In 1979, Chris Hutchins, guitar; Ron Schauf, bass; Kathy Schauf, guitar and vocals; Todd Hidden, drums and vocals, came together to form a third phase of Shine to tour in Wyoming and California.

Photos courtesy: Shine

CLA

Courtesy: CLA

The original CLA formed in 1970 and included John Corkum, vocals; Gary Fessler, guitar; Larry Bally, drums; and Jim Quincy, bass. An early member Max King, proposed the name "Church Life After" that later got shortened to CLA. In part, the acronym paralleled the CTA of the group Chicago. At times, however, there was a running joke that CLA stood for "Crummy Little Amplifiers." During the early 1970s, the band underwent several changes in membership, playing at places like the Stage Door Inn as well as on statewide tours. By 1973-74, CLA focused on dance tunes and consisted of Curt Poole, guitar; Randy Bass, vocals; Brian Dick, keys; Steve Swaim, drums; Curtis Payne, guitar; and Jim Quincy, bass. For a time, Connie White also sang with the group. With Payne and Poole as two major figures, the group was sometimes known as "A tale of two Curts." By 1975, however, various band members went on to pursue their own careers.

Majestic Mood / Tin Ear

Gerald Graves and Larry Bally had been part of the group Majestic Mood, a horn band with Dave Smith on drums, Roger Rudd on bass, and Gary Hoephner as lead singer. Then, they transitioned into a four-piece called Orion, with Alex Isham, guitar; Roger Rudd, bass; Dave Smith, drums; and Gerald Graves, keyboards. When Bally and Rudd left the band, keyboardist Graves looked to form another group. At the time, Bill Landrum was playing with former Jokers member Mike McRoberts and Steve Wilson. Towards the end of 1974, Gerald approached Bill and McRoberts about forming a group with Gerald, Alex and Dave. They agreed and Tin Ear was formed in early 1975. By then, the band consisted of Dave Smith, drums; Alex Isham, guitar; Bill Landrum, bass; and McRoberts and Graves, keyboards. When Dave Smith left the band, Todd Hidden took over on drums and, as Threet recalled, "brought to us a new awareness of the importance of stage presence, presentation and 'antics.'" The band was fairly unique in that it had two keyboard players, Graves and McRoberts.

McRoberts remembered a particularly notable time when they were offered a chance to do a free show at Herman Hill Park on June 15, 1975 (McRoberts' birthday), "They were very excited because this was the hip place to play and party with the audience. We had a great poster made by Bruce Chapman to advertise it. We got to the gig. I turned the organ on and it just warbled and wouldn't get up to pitch. the Minimoog synthesizer didn't work at all. The amps wouldn't work. Somebody from the Parks Department came and examined the electrical outlets. It turned out that rats had eaten through a number of wires, basically rendering the power useless. There were about a thousand people there. We had to tell them all to go home. We did get a great poster out of it."

They mainly played on the road, particularly all over Montana, as well as Rapid City, South Dakota; Peoria, Illinois; and clubs all over Kansas. After a while, they played a few gigs in Wichita, but mostly out of town." Tin Ear followed Legion at the Casino Club in 1975. After that, it was back on the road to the Dakotas and Montana before breaking up about summer 1976.

Legion

Formed in 1972, Legion was the house band at the Casino club until 1975. Featuring: Pat Kelly, drums(1974-'75); Rick Lamb, bass, trombone & vocals; Bryan Hill; Steve Downey, guitar; Chris Church, trumpet & keyboards; Thane Rogers, drums until 1974.

Legion was known for their skill and versatility. Each member could play multiple instruments. This allowed them to do covers of various groups such as the Allman Brothers, Chicago, Edgar Winter and the Doobie Brothers to name a few. Legion played at the Casino club which, for a 3.2 bar, was maybe the largest club in the area.

Photos courtesy: Finnigan & Wood

Finnigan and Wood

Originally from Hutchinson, guitarist Jerry Wood developed a following in Wichita with his band Jerry Wood and the Peggs. Meanwhile, keyboardist Mike Finnigan developed his own following playing with the Serfs and later, with the Jerry Hahn Brotherhood. In 1972, Finnigan joined up with Wood and formed what they called a "kick-ass band that stormed the West Coast and the Midwest." Playing in clubs in Wichita and the Cotillion, the band initially consisted of Michael Finnigan, piano, fender rhodes piano, hammond B3 organ, harmonica, vocals; Jerry Wood, guitar, vocals; David Gates, bass guitar; and Don "Squeek" Cleary, drums, vocals. Lane Tietgen was the band's main songwriter. The band's tours included time in the San Francisco Bay Area including a recording one night, when a young and inexperienced Stephen Barncar made a recording on a 16 track 3M multi-track audio recorder at Wally Heider Studios in San Francisco, resulting in the Blue Thumb album, *Crazed Hipsters*. The album included the songs "Rock And Roll Show," "Highway," "Laughing Eyes," "Tend To Your Own Business," "Hard Times", "Lady Lady," "Death Letter," "My, My, My," "Don't Cry No More," "Down In The Flood." Following the 1972 tour of the bay area, Ray Loeckle joined the band on reeds, tenor sax, keyboards, horn arrangements and Ray "Bags" Bagby was on percussion/drums. Finnigan & Wood was known as a very powerful live band with great vocals, great players, a lot of versatility, and tremendous energy. Finnigan recalled that "we were one of the best anywhere during our short time together," that lasted until 1975, the year that Finnigan left Wichita to pursue a music career in Los Angeles.

The band was inducted into the Kansas Music Hall of Fame in 2012.

Harley Zurrett

Photos courtesy: Russ Oropesa

Formed in 1972, the band consisted of Russ Oropesa as lead singer, Ron Land on rhythm guitar, Steve Wilson on lead guitar, and Mike Foster on bass with "Kansas Dave" Derimus on drums initially, followed later by Fred Hammond. The band played until 1975.

The captain of North High's football team, Oropesa was the lead figure behind the Cyrus Noble Whiskey Band, Southwind, and Tobacco Jones. He worked third shift at Boeing, which allowed him to perform and practice at least five nights a week, even if he had to leave a few gigs early to make it to work on time!

Seagull

Courtesy: Clay Emberson

Seagull did covers but early on began writing their own material. Some of their highlights were warming up for B.W. Stevenson and Dr. Hook's Travelling Medicine show at Henry Levitt Arena.

They were invited to play the Cow Town Ballroom in Kansas City to play a big radio station's yearly broadcast. It was said the broadcast audience was over 400,000. After people called in about them, Good Karma offered them a European tour fronting the Ozark Mountain Daredevils, and if that went well they would get an American tour. Unfortunately, not all members were able to go and they ended up staying home and continued writing and playing.

Paul Goodwin, Hammond organ, Wurlitzer electric piano, acoustic guitar, & vocals; Clay Emberson, lead guitar & vocals; Kraig Noland, lead guitar & vocals; Brett Long, bass & vocals; Lloyd Miller, drums & vocals. Dave Sisk was sound tech, Steve Rush managed.

Sundance

Courtesy: Doug Webb

Bruce Batson was on, bass and vocals; Bat Shunatona on guitar and vocals; Doug Webb, guitar and vocals; John Dondlinger, drums and vocals; and Kip Ehrke, guitar and vocals; and standing, lead singer Chuck Comly.

One of the early Wichita bands to embrace the new blend of country and rock of the early 1970s, Sundance drew their set-list from a combination of soft California country-rock, to traditional honky-tonk and western swing.

For several years the band played around the state as well as gigs in Colorado and Nebraska. In a whirlwind tour of Kansas one-nighters in the early '70s, dubbed, "Mike Finnigan Rides Again," Sundance performed as an opening act for Mike Finnigan and the Dave Mason Band. Later band members included Mike Ehrke and Harry Dobbin.

Puddin' Head

Courtesy: Puddin' Head

This band's story began in the early 1970s with a duet consisting of "Dirty Randy" Shike on guitar and vocals and "Pizza Bob" Goehring on bass, harmonica, trumpet and vocals.

By 1972, they were mainly a rock/folk cover band that played at clubs like So's Your Mother as well as at Herman Hill Park. Adding Kenny Morrison on drums, the group became the "loud rock" cover band Puddin' Head that played at McConnell's officer's club, Joyland, the King Cole Inn, and the Cotillion's battle of the bands.

At one time, the group performed at Herman Hill Park under the name "Bleeding Kansas," in which Pat McJimsey played lead guitar.

Jericho

A band with many names between 1971 and '75, but the one that played in public the most was known as Jericho. They played at Kapaun, Derby High, Andover High, Southeast, East and several private parties. Longtime members were Craig Limbocker, Mark Hornberger, Grant Hartman and Scott Richardson. Others included Jon Elliott, Doug Rhodes and Dave Stewart.

Crank

Photos courtesy: Mark Archibald

Crank formed in 1971 out of the break-up of the Moanin' Glories. The band consisted of Ritchie Kunkle on guitar and vocals; Hoppy Niles on vocals and guitar; Rick Hodge on bass, and Marc Mourning on drums. When the group got together, Niles and Hodge were playing in The Marble Phrogg out of Oklahoma City, where Hodge recalled they were "the wild Led Zep side show with all the hair, hooks, and everything needed to blow our ears out."

Although not a performer, Linda Saffier was an important part of the band as well, serving as "band mother," keeping the band on track for writing music and having a stable source of income.

Crank started out playing at Riverside Park, the Nomar Theater, and "every club, prom, barn dance, anywhere people would listen." Eventually, a meeting was set up with Little John Frederickson, always a great promoter, at a local underground music station for an interview. Shortly after, they were at Cavern Studios in Kansas City recording demos at the same time as the group Kansas.

They became a popular touring band, with Tommy Tuttle and "Tom Across The Street" on staff. They toured from New Mexico to North Dakota, playing with the James Gang, REO SpeedWagon, Frank Zappa, The Hollies and Edgar Winter. In 1972, Mourning left the band and Kenny Morrison joined the group as a drummer. The last gig they played was in Oklahoma City, where they opened for Frank Zappa. By 1975, Kunkle, Hodge, and Saffier had moved to Texas with their families. While Crank played original music in the style of the Stones and Led Zeppelin, Hodge and Kunkle shifted to progressive country music forming a duo called Jezzie. After that, Hodge played with former Moanin' Glory member Karl Berkebile, who had also moved to Texas and remained a well known keyboardist. Hoppy Niles continued to play in Oklahoma and continued as part of Uncle Zep.

Courtesy: Doug Adams

Bandit

About 1973, Doug Adams brought together fellow musicians from Campus High School in Haysville Ks. to form Bandit. The original members were Doug Adams on guitar, Bob Ward on guitar, Rod Vickers on bass guitar and Dave Cassleberry on drums. At first, the group played Sock Hops, school dances, skating rinks and private parties before landing their first house job in 1975, playing at Headfeathers Bar. Eventually, the group played at Sound Sircus, Governors Mansion and other clubs around town.

Bandit also went through member changes at the end of 1975 and early 1976. By then, Tony Amend replaced Ward on guitar, bringing with him a Southern rock influence, as well as skills on the slide guitar. They added a lead singer named Dale Gleason. The group also brought on board keyboardist Wayne Tibbedeaux, a captain in the Air Force. By the middle of 1977, the band split up as members married and moved on to other responsibilities.

The Innkeepers

Courtesy: Fred Bonner

The Innkeepers were the house band at the Penthouse Lounge on the 26th floor of the downtown Holiday Inn. Beginning at the grand opening of the club in 1971 until 1973, the band performed six nights a week. They featured Rick Meyer on sax; Chris Taylor on keyboards; Fred Bonner on drums and Dell Cady on bass.

During their tenure, local musicians sat in with them like guitarists Rick Azim and Greg Skaff. Later members included Skip Schuman, Greg Skaff and James Van Burien.

Soldier

In 1973, several members of Shine formed a new band, Soldier, that consisted of Joe Sauer, guitar and vocals; Ron Schauf, bass; Bob Gilbert, keyboard and vocals; Todd Hidden, drums and vocals; Jerry Sumner, guitars and vocals; Cliff Tipton, guitar and vocals, pedal steel guitar.

At first they played mainly at the Fireside Club, but also performed at the Camelot Club, Stage Door Inn, Sound Sircus, Colony Club. This was one of the busiest times for the musicians, whose colorful matching outfits stood out as the epitome of 1970s band attire!

Photos courtesy: Ron Schauf

Raggs

After "Standard American" disbanded, Bryan Forrester, bass and vocals, and Fred LaMaster keyboards and vocals, formed Raggs to take over as house band at the Scene '70s. Tommy Warren was the guitarist with exacting performances every night. Randy Bradford was the drummer, with Ray Salazar on lead vocals and keyboards. Salazar had his own style and could sing tunes from Bad Company, Todd Rundgren, and even to the high vocals of Yes.

After a couple of years, Randy and Tommy decided it was time to retire. Gary Heitz joined the band as lead guitarist and Todd Hidden eventually settled in on drums and vocals. The band broke up in 1975 when Ray decided to move back home. Fred, Gary and Bryan reunited with Randy Bradford to become the backup band for "The Dean Scott Show," working throughout the U.S. with gigs in Las Vegas and various showrooms around the country. One gig of particular interest was a month-long stint at the Golden Nugget in Las Vegas where the band acted as warmup for Kenny Rogers and B.J. Thomas.

Gandalf

A Progressive Rock band that evolved from the band CLA, Gandalf played from 1973 through 1974 at the Stage Door Inn, Head Feathers, The Yellow Submarine, and the King Cole Inn. Gandalf played covers by Yes, King Crimson, Jethro Tull, among others and were known for their large following. Gandolf was: Lance Threet, guitar, Steve Swaim, drums & vocals; Jim Quincy, bass; John Corkum, lead vocals; Kevin Jones, keyboards.

Betterside

In 1975, Fred Bonner was playing on the road with White River but was tiring of the pace. He now had a young daughter as well and thought it best to develop a more stable way of life back in Wichita. That was when he decided to form a new band for the Brookside Club called the Betterside. This house band consisted of Lloyd Lewis on guitar; Winston Blair on bass; John Kenning on keyboards; and Bonner on drums. Soon after, a variation of the band played at Tom and Sonny's on West Street.

Headstone

Formed by Perry Overstake and Brad Bartlett in 1974, the name came from the head (Rolling) Stone, Mick Jagger. The band included Perry Overstake, bass; Brad Bartlett, drums; Larry Mingle, guitar; Dave Shouse, keyboard; with Louie Garcia and Jaycee Smith on vocals. The manager was Steve Hibler, agent for Studio Talent Associates of Dallas. They toured Kansas, Oklahoma, Iowa, Texas, Missouri and Nebraska. This band was formed primarily as a "Rock/Show Band" with the two singers out front with outfits, and choreography. They covered all kinds of music, from Motown, Rock, Disco and Pop. Some sets were non-stop medleys. Locally, they played in Wichita at The Wild Hare, Sound Sircus, The Casino, The Camelot, The Comedy Club, The Candle Club and others. Members that came through the band included: Bryan Hill, Skip Sangerhausen, Gary Brock, Bonnie Ryder, Curt Poole, Gary House, Kendal Wallace, and Brian Wilson. The band ended in 1985.

Bill Garrison

Cavaliers, from left: Clif Major, Bill Garrison, Pat O'Connor, Bob Brenner
Staff Photo by Jerry Cl

Inspired by the harmonica playing of Sonny Terry, Bill Garrison decided this instrument might just be his calling. Since then, Garrison has played virtually all styles of music—rock and roll, country, blues, bluegrass and jazz.

Once, while standing outside the Kansas blood bank, Garrison's playing made a few people start to dance and that's all it took to set his career path. He was hooked, and began the arduous task of learning the instrument.

When the early 1960s rock bands such as the Beatles, Rolling Stones and Yardbirds began to use the harmonica as an added color, Garrison was frequently seen jamming with the Outcasts and Pat McJimsey.

Forming a duo with Pat O'Conner on piano the pair played all the standard local watering holes such as the foundry and A Black Out. With absolutely no concern for future marketing and branding or the elusive promise of fame and fortune, the duo changed its name for virtually every gig. Once, with the addition of Clif Major on guitar and Bob Brenner on washboard, the group used the moniker "Maurice White and the Cavaliers." Of course there was no Maurice White. Taking the spoof to the limit, the trio was interviewed by the local newspaper where the band members extolled the virtues of Mr. White's vast musical abilities and unparalleled showmanship. Remember, this was long before anyone had heard the term "fake" news.

In the early '70s, Garrison began to accompany himself on guitar and the harmonica went into a rack ala Dylan and Donavan. This is when he began to center his attention on songwriting, a focus he has maintained over the years. Before going solo, Garrison played with several bands including Good Medicine and Tumble Weed.

He has opened for Leon Russell, worked on a CD with Stevie Ray Vaughn's Double Trouble and appeared on KMUW radio. Garrison has self-produced eight CDs of mostly original material and utilizes a stellar cast of local musicians to round out the studio band.

Photos courtesy: Doug Webb

Courtesy: Ron Schauf

Bo Mitchell and Easy Money

In 1974, several of the members of Soldier formed a new band, Bo Mitchell and Easy Money. Calling themselves the "Midwest's Top So-So Rock & Show Band," the group consisted of Cliff Tipton, guitar, vocals, and occasionally drums; Ron Schauf, bass; Bob Mitchell, vocals, Jerry Sumner, guitar and vocals; Todd Hidden, drums; Bob Gilbert, keyboards and vocals. As they had when they were part of Solider and Shine, they played Camelot Club, but also the Wild Hare Club. By now, they had abandoned Soldier's sleek matching outfits and presented a much rougher, grittier image.

Sawdust Charley

Photos courtesy: Harry Dobbin

Formed in the 1970s, country-rock band Sawdust Charley was comprised of Harry Dobbin, bass; Doug Webb, guitar; John Dondlinger, drums; Mike Ehrke, pedal-steel guitar; Jamey Ratzlaff, guitar; and Bob Feldner, sound engineer. The bands playlist was predominately original material, with songwriting responsibilities handled by virtually every member of the band. This variety of writing styles and vocal treatments gave the group a versatility few other acts could rival. The band took special pride in its musicianship, well-crafted harmonies, strong rhythm section and song arranging ability, with the final product often going well beyond the songwriter's greatest expectations.

By the mid-1970s, Sawdust Charley's music was in regular rotation on KFDI FM radio and the band was listed as one of its most requested acts. The band worked many special promotions with the radio station as well working roadhouses, ballrooms, bars around the Midwest. It was not uncommon for Wichita die-hard Sawdust Charley fans to travel several hundred miles to attend the band's out-of-town gigs. In addition to regular road work the band opened for such luminaries as Asleep at the Wheel, The Earl Scruggs Review and the Ozark Mountain Daredevils.

Hometown gigs were viewed as special occasions and the band never failed to pack local clubs and bars, including numerous capacity crowds at the 2,100 seat Cotillion Ballroom.

In 1978, the band relocated to southern California in search of recording opportunities. While there, the band won the talent contest at the Palomino Club and performed at the prestigious Troubadour in Los Angeles. The band played jobs around California, Oregon and Wyoming and performed at the world famous Million Dollar Cowboy Bar in Jackson Hole.

Road weary, disillusioned and facing a rapidly changing musical demographic, Sawdust Charley hung up their spurs in 1979.

Sawdust Charley was inducted into the Kansas Music Hall of Fame in 2016.

Courtesy: Terry Hacker

Axis / Shady Oak Bombers

In the late 1960s, Steve Downey, Terry Hacker, and Thane Rogers formed the band Axis, taking the name from the album "Axis Bold as Love" by Jimi Hendrix. This version of the band, playing in the basement of Steve Downey's mother, did not last long. A new version emerged with Hacker on bass and Downey on guitar, joined by Norman Mehl on Hammond B-3 and Pat Kelly on drums. By 1969, Downey and Rogers had become part of Legion, the house band at the Casino. Axis reformed again to consist of Steve House, and Ron Barnhart, lead vocals and trumpet, Mike Kilpatrick on guitar, Thane Rogers on drums and Terry Hacker on bass. At one time John Smith and Kenny Williams were on guitar, with Steve Railing and Dave Smith on drums. By then the band played clubs like the Spot and Foundry 21. They had started to develop a reputation for what the local paper called "a fusion of funk, heavy rock, and southern rock overtones. "The same article noted that," the group wrote its own music but also played "everything from Steely Dan to Marshall Tucker…" and "one of the most impressive things about the group, aside from the oh, so nice way they play together is that each is a strong soloist."

Photos courtesy: Kip Ehrke

James Brothers Band

The James brothers - David, bass; Fred, guitar and Chris, keyboards - were raised in a musical environment. Their father, Alfred James III, a geologist and part-time jazz musician exposed the sons to a wide range of musical genres through his involvement with The Wichita Jazz Festival, KMUW and the jazz club Bill's Le Gourmet.

Fred James, the eldest brother, was first to hit the Wichita music scene in the mid-1970s, but was soon followed by his brothers Chris and David. The three were soon playing in various bands with other well-known local musicians such as Pat McJimsey, Clif Major, Greg Skaff, Larry Chaney, Bill Hawks, Kip Ehrke and John Salem.

In January of 1978, after moving to Nashville, Fred released a solo album. With a desire to make it a family business, Chris and David soon relocated to Nashville and with the addition of two other Wichita musicians, drummer, Chuck Comley, and multifaceted Jerry Wood formed the James Brothers Band.

Over the years, the James brothers continued to tour and record. Fred and Chris play in the Burrito Brothers band.

The Jesse James Band in 1976 - Fred James, Chris James, Doug James, Larry Chaney, and Kip Ehrke.

Image

Courtesy: David Fleming

"The largest light and sound show on the road," Image formed in 1975. The band's first promoter and manager was underground DJ, Little John Fredrickson. Later, Larry Jones and his father, J.C., formed Imagination Productions to manage the band.

The band recruited from among local musicians. Singers included Bob McFarlane and Willie Nunez. Guitarists included Roger Jones, David Fleming, Kevin Brown, Scott Lee, Don Berry, Scott Reed, and Bob Budavich. Mark Brownlee was the key bassist, along with Don Berry, Charlie Donahue, David Fleming, and Jerry Rogers. Keyboardists included Darrell Page, Dave Moulton, and Charlie Donahue. Drummers were Shawn Jennings, Doug Nelson, Jerry Pond, Mick Grim, "Critter," Steve Brasewell, Mike Bradley, Stan Hartman, Woodie Schrader, Tony Gable and Mike Baptist. This turnover in membership meant that Image never developed a signature sound. Its signature was unusual outfits and show equipment crammed into the back of a converted bus. Equipment required the technical support of soundman Chris Locke and roadies such as Tom Collins and Chris Bell.

Thesis

Courtesy: Mike Metz

This band's story began in the late 1960s with a group of friends from Goddard High School: Kent Havener, Jeff Frey and Dave Clothier. Clothier and Havener, along with Shannon McGinness, had formed a short-lived garage band that played a few parties and sock hops. After the breakup of that group, they met Mike Metz. They practiced at Mike's house and, as Dave Clothier recalled, "his parents, Gerald and Phyllis Metz, were really supportive, and did a lot of driving for the band before any of us had a license. Mike's basement was a great place to practice, and Mike had a workshop next to the band area that he started his career in electronics in. I remember him building a PAIA synthesizer from a kit way before you could buy one at a music store."

The group called itself Thesis and was a regular feature at the King Cole Inn, Yellow Submarine, Harolds Club and Herman Hill Park. It also performed at the Comedy Club and school dances. Regarding the type of music played, Metz recalled that "we did a bit of everything rock, UFO, Slade, Captain Beefheart, Yardbirds, Blue Oyster Cult, ZZ Top, Zeppelin, Wishbone Ash, J. Geils."

Over time, the band featured three distinct lineups. Lasting from 1969 through 1976, the first lineup consisted of Kent Havener, guitar; Dave Clothier, bass; Jeff Frey, vocals; and Mike Metz, drums. By the late 1970s, the band had changed slightly. Clothier left in 1973 to attend St. John's Military School followed by the University of Kansas (and, a few years later, returned to Wichita to help form the Shi(r)theads. Steve White replaced Clothier on bass. In 1976, Mike Metz opened Thesis Audio Service and focused more on touring with this and other bands as a sound and lights tech. By the early 1980s, a third version had taken shape with Ralph Padilla and Ken Peoples, guitar; Steve White, bass; and Mike Metz, drums.

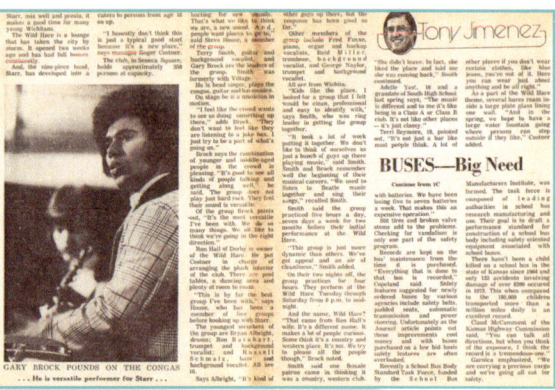
Courtesy: Starr

Starr

Starr initially consisted of Gary Brock on lead vocals, Terry Smith on guitar, Al Rowe on keyboards, Mike Kittel on drums and Ron Barnhardt and Steve House on horns. Starr had a house gig at a club in the lower level of Seneca Square called The Wild Hare. The group underwent a change in 1974, when three members of the former band Boogie joined the group. Bill Wullschleger replaced Brock on vocal and Kittel on drums, Curt Poole replaced Smith on guitar, and Norman Mehl on keyboards. Terry Hacker, himself a former Boogie member, played bass.

Courtesy: Jim Hill

Sideways

Formed in the late 1970s and performing mainly at the Tennessee Gin Mill and Beer Mill, Sideways consisted of Lloyd Miller, drums; Jim Hill, guitar; Steve Balduff, guitar; and Stephen Williams, bass, vocals. Jim Hill recalled that "we tried to play songs that not every other band in Wichita played. We played stuff by groups like, 10cc, Steely Dan, Gino Vanelli, and other groups like that."

Traveller

Formed 1976, Traveller was Jon Weaver on guitar and banjo, Toby Fisher on guitar, Gene Turner on bass, Tony Gable on drums, Matt McClintock as lead vocalist, and Paul Zumwald on keys. This band played at The Tennessee Gin Mill and Tennessee Beer Mill. They also played the Coyote Club and the various Foundry Clubs in Wichita. They toured around Kansas playing many of the small town venues. During this time, DJ music was coming into its own, making it harder for bands to compete price wise. So groups started diversifying and blending rock and country. Traveller did this as well and in time, Weaver left to become part of the country group Oklahoma Sunshine.

Tumbleweed/Windfall

In the early 1970s, a group of musicians from the University of Kansas scene formed a band called Mud Pie. A number of venues kept confusing them with a more popular group called Mud Creek, so, by 1973, the band had renamed itself Tumbleweed. The band consisted of various members over time, beginning with Vicki Childers, guitar, mandolin and vocals; Mark Palmer, guitar and vocals; and John Stewart, bass and vocals. Later members were Mark Dannar, guitar; Kirk Sorensen, guitar, harmonica, and violin; Bill Garrison, guitar, harmonica and percussion; and Brad Schulz, drums. In 1975, the group learned that another band had already trademarked that name so they renamed themselves Windfall. At that point, the lineup included Childers, Palmer, Stewart, and Schulz.

The group covered material by Bonnie Raitt, Joni Mitchell, Van Morrison, the Grateful Dead, Jim Croce, and others. The group lasted until about 1975, with several members going on to form the group Alias the following year.

Courtesy: Lickety Split

Lickety Split

Forming in 1975, Lickety Split occupied the gig as house band for the Stage Door Inn. Performing 70s staples from varying bands such as Kool & The Gang, The Ohio Players to Deep Purple and Jethro Tull. Lickety Split took advantage of singer John Corkum's ability to imitate and cover many different singers and styles. Lickety Split was; John Corkum, vocals; Lance Threet, guitar; Jerry Summer, drums, Ron Schauf, bass; Kevin Jones, keyboards.

Mediaevil

Formed in the mid 1970s, Mediaevil consisted of Tom Wheeler on guitar, Woody Schrader on drums and piano; Bruce Stevens (followed by Bud Mitchner) on bass, and John Corkum, vocals. Corkum and Mitchner had known each other since their Smokey Bear band days. Known for a "Mod Punk" sound, the group was inspired by the music of Peter Gabriel and, at times at least, the look of the emerging punk scene. Mediaevil played at the Beer Mill as well as clubs, dances and private parties. Looking back on the those times, Corkum was amazed that playing two nights a week could net $400 to $600. The group lasted until about 1979 when Tom Wheeler moved out of town.

Sunset

Sunset formed in 1971 with three musicians who played with the Lost Souls: Curt Poole, guitar; Bill Harrel, bass; and Lloyd Miller, drums. Poole and Harrel had been with "Lo & Behold," while Miller was previously with the group "Camel." Harrel soon left and joined the Velvet Rainbow, while Poole and Miller stayed on with a series of other guitarists including Gary Wall, Fred James, & Jerry Sumner.

By then the group transformed into Sunset. Meanwhile, Miller went on to play with Seagull, and was replaced by Todd Hidden on drums.

Sunset played popular rock songs by groups of the day like James Gang, the Beatles, the Who, Cream, Badfinger, the Byrds, Jethro Tull, Savoy Brown - along with unusual rock arrangements of folk ballads & old country songs for dancing. Sunset was one of the first bands to play at Herman Hill Park.

Jake

An early '70s band, that was "short-lived but hot stuff," Jake brought together musicians who had been with some of Wichita's most popular bands such as the Outcasts, the Prophets, and Lion's Mane. The Lineup included Darryl Osburn, vocals; Clif Major, guitar and banjo; Steve McCaskie, bass; Danny Personne, drums; and Greg Skaff, guitar. Playing "blues-tinged rock and country," they took their inspiration from the Rolling Stones, Grateful Dead, Muddy Waters, Johnny Cash, Leadbelly, Dylan, and Buffy St.Marie. Among the venues that they played were the Nomar Theater and The Phone Booth.

Polite Force

The initial line up of Polite Force included Jerry Sumner, drums; Lance Threet, guitar; Kevin Jones, keyboards; and Jeff Stevenson, bass. When Jones and Stevenson left, Threet and Sumner then joined Sir Cuss. Sir Cuss had already been around for a few years before and consisted of Larry Bally, Jim Quincy, Gerald Graves, Clay Emberson, and Jackie Keimig. Towards the end of that group, Emberson and Keimig quit and Threet and Sumner took their place. Sir Cuss ended when Bally and Quincy decided they were not able to tour and Threet, Sumner and Graves formed a new band, using again the name Polite Force. Initially, Paul Slagle and then Reggie Littleton were on bass. After Littleton left, Sumner became the bass player with Russ Weiss on drums for a time, followed by Todd Hidden. Threet recalled that Hidden "came aboard with the new 'presentation awareness,' things began to move in a positive direction. Hidden raised the caliber of the band and when he left, set the stage for Steve Swaim to join and start the group's transition into the Clocks.

Sahara

Courtesy: Sahara

In the early 1970s, Doug Walker was a music student at Wichita State University, learning under the guidance of Jerry Hahn (who advised him one time that "if you make a mistake, just play it seven times and people will think you are adding tension to the music." His local music contacts came to include Pat McJimsey and Walker played with the Entire British Navy for a time. In 1973, Walker, joined with a group of musicians to form the band Sahara.

Sahara consisted of Doug Walker on guitar, Ron Black; vocals and percussion (including congas); Steve Braswell on drums; Joe Horton on keyboard, and David Winter on bass, a role that Keith Messer later filled. Mike Metz, who was with Thesis Audio, served as soundman. Metz's skills as a repairman ensured the equipment was in good order.

Sahara's members insisted on being willing to play "anything and everything." This would mean Top 40 and progressive rock, but it also could include blues and jazz, ranging from John Coltrane to Chick Corea. The band played a set of familiar tunes and then switched to something so unusual, that the audience later came up to asked "who was that you were playing?" Sahara prided itself on being a band's band and enjoyed educating the general public on new music as well as the challenge of playing really complicated, difficult work.

The band played jazz festivals, a variety of clubs including the Foundry Downtown, Yellow Submarine, and the Barcelona Club, a short-lived club that catered mainly to airmen from McConnell Air Force Base. At one supper club, Sahara played three sets, one low key music for the dinner hour, followed by a Top 40 dance set, and then a cutting-edge collection of jazz works. A few patrons stayed for all three sets. The band did some touring to Nebraska and Oklahoma, finding that the variety of their music range allowed them to make as much in a few nights of playing as some band did playing the grind of six nights a week.

Sahara lasted until the middle 1970s, when Walker moved to Kansas City. He found that Wichita had a much more active and accomplished music scene than Kansas City. The other members stayed on in Wichita, with Metz, for example, continuing to play drums for Thesis.

Courtesy: Ron Schauf

Balloon Warfare

After Likety-Split ended in 1975, Ron Schauf played various gigs before joining with Jim Hill, Steve Balduff, and Steve Swaim to form Balloon Warfare. The group consisted of Jim Hill, vocals and guitar; Ron Schauf, bass and vocals; Steve Balduff, guitar; Steve Swaim, drums and vocals. Getting their start playing at a friend's wedding, they went on to play Herman Hill Park, Governeour's Mansion, the Colony Club, Rathskeller Club and the Stage Door Inn. Calling itself a "contemporary rock-dance group," they played songs from performers as varied as the Beatles, Steely Dan and Stevie Wonder.

Oklahoma Sunshine Band

Oklahoma Sunshine Band was among the first country rock groups to perform in Wichita. Vince Baker recalled that the band formed in 1976, with Don Neal, Vince Baker and Chuck Haukus. Baker noted that "Our first gig was at the Monterey Club in Winfield. We named the band Oklahoma Sunshine because I still had old posters from a previous short-lived band." They posted them on almost every telephone pole between Wichita and Winfield. Don and Chuck would take turns on bass and lead guitar. The band took another turn when they hired a fiddle player named Chuck Turner thus adding a Charlie Daniels effect. He was in the Air Force and was shipped to Washington State. At about the same time they hired the fiddle player, they happened on Jeff Pickering at Mac's Guitar Studio and approached him and asked him if he would be interested in playing in a progressive country band. He said yes and he remained with the band. The band decided to turn over the running of the band to Dave Reed, the new bassist that had more business knowledge and took the band to new heights. Over the years, the band had a lot of changes in personnel but remained true to its sound, at that time they called it Progressive Country.

The band consisted, at various times, of Don Neal on guitar and vocals; Vince Baker on drums; Jeff Pickering on pedal steel guitar, rhythm guitar, banjo, fiddle, and vocals; Jon Weaver on guitar, Dave Reed on bass guitar and vocals; Bryan Driscoll on guitar and mandolin; Gary Wall on guitar; Matt McClintock on drums, bass, and vocals; and Scott Abbott on bass and vocals. The band was capable of playing old country and outlaw country as well as country rock and southern rock for that audience. OSB sometimes drew odd looks from traditional country crowds at first because of their long hair and scruffy appearance. Meanwhile, rock audiences sometimes didn't know what to make of the pedal steel on the bandstand at first. OSB also put out a 45 RPM record. One side was "Shady Lady" written by Jeff Pickering. The other side was "The Teaser" both were sung by Don Neal. Baker noted that "we ordered a thousand copies and gave them all away."

Cyrus Noble Whiskey Band

Named for a brand of whiskey sold in Kansas in the 1890s, the band consisted of Russ "Big O" Oropesa as lead singer, Bill Shumate on lead guitar, Lynn Piller on rhythm and steel guitar, Barry Clark on rhythm guitar and harp, Mike Foster on bass, and Don "Squeek" Clarey on drums.

From 1976 through 1980, the band was a staple at the Admiral's in Park City as well as the Spot and the Overflow in Wichita. The band also played outdoor concerts at Herman Hill Park, one of which was the week before the infamous Herman Hill Riot of April 1979.

Cats Cradle

Cats Cradle existed for a short time. Guitar and vocals were from Curtis Payne, who had recently left CLA. Other members were Dale Gleason on lead vocals, Woody Schrader on drums; Kyle Pinkerton on bass, and Brian Dick on keyboards. The group played a lot of radio hits but lasted only a few months, with only one gig at the Heidelberg Inn in Augusta, Kansas. Curtis, Brian and Woody left to pursue original music in the vein of Emerson, Lake and Palmer. For a time, they recruited Brad Ulrich on bass for that short lived no name project.

Courtesy: Curtis Payne

Manilla Road

Courtesy: Manilla Road

In 1977, heavy metal was starting to be popular among a group of students at North High, who formed a band called Embryo with Mark Shelton on drums and Jim Stark on guitar. Shelton then went into the Marines and upon returning, developed Manilla Road with Ben Munkirs on drums, Scott Park on bass and Shelton on guitar. Inspired by the stage performances of KISS, the group played with sound and light equipment and pyrotechnics initially under the guidance of Allen Denny.

After Munkirs left the group, Myles Sype became drummer, followed by Rick Fisher. Unlike most bands, Manilla Road played only original music, with Shelton writing lyrics, inspired by science fiction and fantasy writing. Manilla Road recorded a demo, *Manilla Road Underground*, with three songs titled "Far Side of the Sun", "Herman Hill" and "Manilla Road." By 1979, the group recorded their first album, *Invasion*, on their own label Roadster Records. They even did a live radio broadcast from the local university station KMUW-FM. The group then went on to record three more albums, *Dreams of Eschaton*, (later called *Mark of the Beast*), *Metal* and *Crystal Logic*.

The albums got national and international play. By 1983, a Dutch radio station voted *Crystal Logic* as the best album of the year. They did their own distribution and promotion from their own label but had started making contacts in a couple of countries in Europe. Crystal Logic had been received so well in parts of Europe that the band drew the attention of an up-and-coming label called Black Dragon Records, which released *Open The Gates*, followed by *The Deluge*, *Mystification*, *Live Roadkill*, *Out of the Abyss* and *The Courts of Chaos*. The band also toured the U.S., with Randy Thrasher Foxe replacing Rick Fisher.

By the 1990s, Manilla Road had disbanded and Shelton formed a new group, Circus Maximus. His prior group's success, however, was such that Circus Maximus recorded an album with Black Dragon as a Manilla Road piece. In the years since, Shelton and Foxe have reconstituted Manilla Road and have appreciated their fan base, which is even stronger in Europe than in the United States. Looking back, Shelton recalled, "I know that Manilla Road does not appeal to everyone, even in the metal world. And our production style is a bit archaic and definitely different than most. But that is part of the mystique of the band and the music. I have and always will treat my music like a mad scientist in the lab. Experimentation is the key to finding the elusive lost chord. Music is magic and without magic we are nevermore."

Sweetwater Band

Photos courtesy: Doug Adams

Following the break up of Bandit, Doug Adams formed a new band with piano player and singer Paula Travis, guitarist Jerry Hinson, and bass player Mike Maxey. Maxey brought in Pat Keitel as drummer. The group named itself the Sweetwater Band to distinguish itself from another band called Sweetwater.

The Sweetwater Band's first gig was at Governor's Mansion on March 18, 1978. The next week Pete Seaton invited the group to become the house band for his new club, the Tennessee Gin Mill. For the next several years, the group played seven nights a week, mostly at the Tennessee Gin Mill and Beer Mill. Other gigs included Sunday performances at Herman Hill Park, even performing shortly before the infamous riot on April 15, 1979.

By the late 1970s, the band membership changed with Jimmy Baker replacing Pat Keital as drummer; Rod Vickers replacing Mike Maxey on bass; and Tony Amend replacing Paula Travis on vocals. In 1981 the group opened a show at the Cotillion for rock legend John Kay & Steppenwolf.

The Sweetwater Band lasted until 1982. Doug Adams began working as a sound man for Oklahoma Sunshine, The Clocks, Dogs? and many others, resulting in Pro Audio Systems, Inc. Since 1989, Adams has been the stage manager and sound engineer for John Kay & Steppenwolf.

Courtesy: Gerald Graves

Sir Cuss

Formed in the mid 1970s, Sir Cuss was mainly a touring band that played gigs across Kansas, Oklahoma and Nebraska. Known for playing contemporary rock standards like those of Peter Frampton and Steely Dan, the group consisted of guitarists Clay Emberson and Jackie Keimig; Larry Bally on drums; Jim Quincy on bass, and Gerald Graves on keyboards. As Quincy recalled, "in the first year we dressed like normal musicians." Then, the group switched to a "stage drag look with flashy clothes and showy performances and "we doubled our money." When Emberson and Keimig quit, Lance Threet and Jerry Sumner joined. With Graves as the main coordinator, the band at first traveled just in the immediate region. By 1977, Threet, Graves, and Sumner were interested in more extensive touring, an interest that resulted in the end of Sir Cuss and the three forming the core of the second version of Polite Force, a group that would later become the Clocks.

Slip

When Balloon Warfare had ended, Ron and Kathy Schauf looked for a new set of musicians with which to play. In the summer 1978, they met up with Kim Koffman and Chris Hutchen and began to practice together. By the end of the year, Slip had formed. The band's tenure was short lived, however, ending in March when Kim quit the group and setting the stage for Kathy Schauf, Ron Schauf, and Chris Hutchens to join with Todd Hidden to form Shine. The band played two original songs written by Kathy Schauf: "Universal Song" and "Hidden."

The group played at Governeour's Mansion and the Beer Place, They played their last gig at the Foundry West in early 1979, which Ron Schauf recalled was "the best job we ever had."

Storm

Storm began with an invitation from Alan Banta to Arthur Glass to come to his parent's house and jam. Both attended Robinson Junior High and met in Algebra class. They discovered their mutual interest in starting a band.

The original plan was to play in the garage, but there was severe weather so the jam session was moved to the basement. Alan had a pawn shop guitar and a non-descript tube amp. Arthur arrived with a drum kit he bought for $25 on the way to Alan's. In the weeks to come, the two got together twice a week and invited friends and acquaintances to join. Since the sky darkened and the sirens wailed so many nights they got together, the players began to joke that they were the cause and Storm was born. One of their signatures for opening concerts was the song "Riding the Storm Out."

In the fall, Alan and Arthur started high school at Southeast and East, respectively. They extended the invitation to join a band to their new classmates. One of the first to accept was Lee McCroskey playing keyboards. The qualifications were that you had to play an instrument, sing or have the rock star look. Like most bands, the songs Storm learned were covers of 50s and 60s rock tunes. Those early line ups leaned toward guitar driven, rock and roll, but with the growing popularity of bands like Chicago, Blood, Sweat and Tears and the Ohio Players an idea emerged. Soon, Clark Engbrecht joined the group playing trumpet, and Kevin Smith on trombone. Dick Duncan joined the group as lead singer, forming the nucleus of the group that would last for decades. Throughout their high school years, Storm played gigs at private parties and became particularly popular playing Junior High sock hops. (Yes, they still existed.) The kids who attended those parties essentially grew up with the band and followed the group for years. All of the band members graduated high school in the Spring of 1975. That summer, they meet Bob Freeman, a bass player from Pratt, KS. After a WSU parking lot jam session showed off Bob's skills, he became Storm's full time bass player, and created the '75 - '79 line up.

Photos courtesy: Alan Banta

The Embarrassment

Formed in 1979, The Embarrassment was one of Wichita's most successful punk rock bands. It consisted of Bill Goffrier, vocals and guitar; John Nichols, vocals & organ; Ron Klaus, bass; Brent "Woody" Giessmann, drums. Goffrier, Nichols, and Giessmann had formed a trio back in 1977 with a group known as The Lemurs and then The Spontanes. With the addition of Klaus, they began performing and recording as The Embarrassment, nicknamed "The Embos."

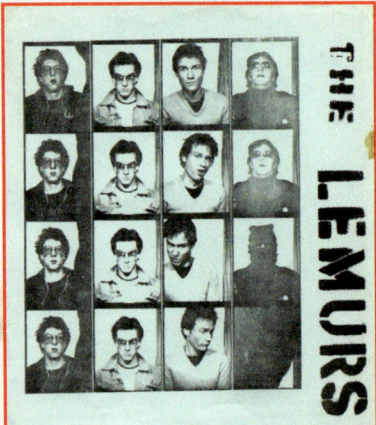

In 1979, they recorded at Hi Fidelity Studios a set of songs including "Sex Drive", "After The Disco", "Pushin' Too Hard", "Patio Set", and "Berliner's Night Out". This was the first of several recording sessions that followed. The band toured and performed steadily until 1983 when Goffrier and Giessmann moved to Boston, leading to careers with major label bands Del Fuegos and Big Dipper. Their most recent reunion was 2006 in Wichita. The album *Heyday*, released in 1995, highlights their 1979-1983 music career.

Photos courtesy: the Embarrassment

Tobacco Jones

From 1981 through 1983, this country rock band included Russ Oropesa as lead vocalist, George Mueller and Jeff Smith on guitars, Mike Foster and Dan Carmichael on bass and Russ Oropesa on drums. The band's name was a take off on the catch phrase "Basketball Jones" and was a regular feature at the King Cole Inn, the Spot, and the Foundry.

They even played two concerts at the Kansas State Industrial Reformatory in Hutchinson, the only concerts they played that had an all-male audience.

Photos courtesy: Russ Oropesa

Courtesy: Curtis Payne

The Dive Kings

The one thing the Dive Kings could not tolerate was audience indifference—either love them or hate them. The band was fueled by audience reaction which led to many great performances as well as some outrageous onstage behavior. The Dive Kings have been described as Animal House with guitars.

Formed in 1978, the original band was called Weekend Wally and included Curtis Payne, guitar; Bob Gilbert, keyboards; Phil Nelson, bass; Michael Penney, sax; and Larry Bally, drums. However, playing current pop covers of the day was quickly proving to be a dead-end pursuit. Working bands were quickly being replaced with drum machines, synthesizers and sequencers. In fact, a DJ with a few turn tables could satisfy the dance whims of the largest crowd.

In an attempt to find their muse, Weekend Wally decided to learn one set of material from their 1960s youth—Soul, Psychedelic and Rhythm and Blues. For added emphasis, the band dressed in '60s attire
The first outing for the Dive Kings—a name attributed to Curtis Payne—was a company Christmas party where the band was a huge hit. However, not all of their gigs went so swimmingly. During their first appearance at the Cotillion Ballroom, the band was booed off the stage. In retaliation, they did the only thing any respectable rock & roll band could do—they trashed the dressing room. The group was banned from the Cotillion; however, this act of aggression only fueled their reputation as a raucous, must-see act. Eventually, the ban was lifted and the Dive Kings have maintained a good relationship with the Cotillion over the years.

After the incident at the Cotillion, drummer Larry Bally left the band and was replaced by Jim Hill in 1979. When Bally returned to the drum kit Jim Hill moved to guitar. In 1980, the membership was finalized with the addition of Kate Nelson on trumpet and Pat Jennings, vocals.

The Dive Kings set list covered a spectrum that ranged from Wilson Pickett to Paul Revere and the Raiders, and the Blues Magoos.

Performing all over the Midwest the band also opened for many top acts such as Delbert McClinton, the Turtles, the Grass Roots and Wilson Pickett.

In 1981 the band recorded an album they sold from the stage at various performances. The album also was distributed across the east coast and resulted in a mention in Billboard magazine.

The group broke up in 1990 and briefly reformed in 2000. To the delight of their many fans, the band has had several reunion gigs over the years.

Mini Max

Courtesy: Mini Max

Mini Max began as a duo consisting of Bryan Hill on drums and Doug Terbush on organ, key bass, lead vocal. They were a very popular jazz/pop group that performed at The Camelot Club, an upstairs private club on east side of Wichita. Terbush and Hill then invited Richard Lamb and Robin "Chris" Church to join them, Lamb and Church feeling like they had joined the big leagues. This larger Mini Max consisted of Doug Terbush, organ, key bass, lead vocal; Bryan Hill drums; Richard Lamb, trombone; and Robin "Chris" Church, trumpet. The group lasted only about four months and played only at the Camelot Club. They played 10 p.m. - 2 a.m. four nights a week, which was brutal for the three members who were attending WSU. Mini Max broke up when Terbush decided to try a solo career and the rest of the group went on to play with The Board of Regents.

Dewy & The Big Dogs

Photos courtesy: Dewy & the Big Dogs

Dewy & The Big Dogs formed in 1982 and lasted until 2006. Featuring Sheldon Coleman, guitars and vocals; Chris Griffith, drums and vocals; Bob Howse, vocals and keyboards; Lynn Pillar, guitars and vocals' Cliff "Bo" Reusch, bass and vocals; Scott Piper, guitar and vocals. Referred to as "Dewy" by Chris Griffith who was employed by a construction company ran by Sheldon Coleman before the Big Dogs were formed. Coleman started The Big Dogs in the early 1980s after living in California during the 1970s and being exposed to the energetic alt-rock scene on the West Coast. The band would translate that into the innovative and energetic guitar-driven dance music much of the decade was known for.

Through Lynn Pillar, the "driver" of the band, The Big Dogs played original songs and covers that featured the talent and versatility of the bands members. Their covers of Billy Idol, ZZ Top, The Pretenders and the Police were among the bands "bread and butter" performances. A band of versatile musicians, Coleman also was the promoter of the band and had the business savvy to keep the "Big Dogs' at the front of the Wichita music scene during the 80s. Using a continuously updated mailing list, holding weekly drawings prizes for hats, jackets and t-shirts (even a Coleman canoe one week!), and frequent airplay, the band was heavily promoted.

The Big Dogs could be found playing live weekly at venues such as The Grape, The Hatch, Boogies, Big Dog Studios (inside Roxy's downtown), the Lettuce Club and of course the Coyote Club. In addition to their prolific Wichita presence, the Big Dogs also had national attention as they released a 45, then a full album *Corporate Rock* and later a CD titled *New Tricks*. A video was shot for the single "Corporate Rock" which was produced by local musician John Salem and his production company. The video was shot in the Misco building in Wichita and received brief airtime on MTV.

Redshirt

By the 1980s, many musicians who had honed their craft in the early days of rock & roll began to feel alienated from the post-punk era and emerging MTV generations. Some looked back at their roots for inspiration. One such group was Redshirt—comprised of four members of the defunct Sawdust Charley, plus a former founding member of the Outcasts—found this music to be just the tonic needed to revive the rock & roll doldrums. Redshirt played Century II for the 1985 Big Reunion and backed up the Soule Survivors and Mike Finnigan. They also opened shows with Rick Nelson.

The band included Harry Dobbin, bass and vocals; Doug Webb, guitar; John Dondlinger, drums; Mike Ehrke, guitar and vocals and Jim Kent, keyboards and vocals.

Photos courtesy: Harry Dobbin

The Kozmen

Formed in Wichita in 1978, the Kozmen made a demo tape and soon became a road band, touring Colorado, Wyoming, Texas, Arkansas, Louisiana, and Arizona, and venues such as Mr. Lucky's in Denver. They also opened for many bands with recording contracts such as The Guess Who, Alice Cooper, Shooting Star, Whitford Saint Holmes, and others. Part of the "glam rock," "hair band" trend, their concerts included plenty of light shows and explosions. The original band consisted of Chris Hutchens, backing vocals and lead guitar; Jim Hutchens, lead singer; David Ira, guitar, and Greg Knopke, bass. In the years that followed, the band changed a number of members. The most significant change, however, took place when Ira left and the group transformed itself into a three piece band called the Distractors that lasted until 1982.

Denim

The house band at the Cypress Club and the Crystal Pistol Club, Denim played everything from Southern rock to funk in the years between 1979 and 1981. The members were Kevin Brown, lead guitar and vocals; Roy Whetstone, bass and vocals; Michael Davis, drums and vocals; Rick Scudder vocals, and Terry Hacker, bass and vocals. They played mostly at clubs but also for private parties. Guitarist Kevin Brown recalled that, "we were very busy and played every weekend." Rick Scudder left the band in 1981 and the group continued to play for about another 10 months or so as a three-piece band.

Courtesy: the Dogs?

Dogs?

Dogs? formed in Wichita around 1980, with Joe McWhorter on keyboards and lead vocals, Randy Fields on bass and lead vocals, Conrad Stolze on guitar. Tony Sanford was on drums, followed by Steve Braswell and Stan Hartman. Meanwhile Doug Kimball took over on bass followed by Barry Dirks. Hartman and Dirks also sang until Jay Wetzler came on board. Dogs? then recorded a five song EP. They performed as The Stand on a tour in Canada and for a short time in Kansas. When Wetzler left and Jerry Sumner joined, the band decided to change the name back to Dogs? Sumner recut all the vocal tracks on the still unreleased EP, which came out in 1984. The band also appeared in the low budget horror flick "Night Screams" in 1985, though only as a "stunt band" synched up to pre-recorded music. Dogs? played in Wichita and across Kansas. Dogs? also holds the unique distinction of opening for not one, but two, wrestling bears. The band performed and picked up some label interest into the mid-1980s but creative differences moved the members on to different endeavors. Several of the members showed up together in different regional acts and came together for several reunion shows in 2009 and 2011.

Dawayne Bailey

Courtesy: Dawayne Bailey

In the bustling Wichita music scene of the mid-1970s, Dawayne Bailey was considered a "must see" guitar player. Bailey played with a host of local bands including Fathers and Sons with Craig "Twister" Steward, Vonna Faye and Hot Koffee, the Rising Sons, Show & Tell, Jack Black and Masque. In addition to his well-known guitar prowess, Bailey plays piano, pedal-steel guitar, as well as being a talented singer and gifted songwriter.

In his time on the Wichita stage he performed in virtually every bar, restaurant, and dive as well as the Cotillion Ballroom and the Kansas Coliseum. In 1982, Bailey was asked to join Bob Seger and the Silver Bullet Band and from 1983 to 1986 he toured and recorded with this band. Bailey can be heard on Seger's "Like a Rock" television commercials for Chevy trucks. By the mid-'80s, Bailey returned to Wichita from California and had formed his own band Private Parts, which briefly included backup vocalist Martina (Schiff) McBride.
In 1986, Bailey began to tour and record with the legendary band Chicago and remained with the band until 1995. Bailey also participated in Chicago's 1993 ceremony of the band receiving their star on the Hollywood Walk Fame. Bailey has worked extensively in television and film and was inducted into the Kansas Music Hall of Fame in 2007.

The Clocks

The story of the Clocks began with Jerry Sumner and Lance Threet as friends at Curtis Junior High. When they transitioned to Southeast High, they met up with Gerald Graves. The three then went on to perform in bands during the 1970s including a second version of Polite Force. What set them apart from the other bar bands of the era, however, was their New Wave sound. By 1979, this second version of Polite Force was preparing to become a touring band. The group had added first Todd Hidden, and later, Steve Swaim on drums. Sumner recalled in the Wichita Eagle, that Swaim "came up with some pretty commercial, straight-ahead stuff, and then we got hooked up with CBS and got a deal. So we went to L.A. and did all that stuff."

With the help of Rick Nielsen of Cheap Trick, the Clocks were signed by CBS records on a Boulevard/CBS label that yielded two minor hits with "19" and "She Looks a Lot Like You." Another single, "Summer," received a lot of airplay and "She Looks a Lot Like You," made it to No. 67 on the Billboard Charts. The Clocks' greatest success was when they filmed a video for "She Looks a Lot Like You," in a whirlwind session in Monterey, California, which made its way onto MTV. MTV had just launched the music video as a concept and was still playing these to a few test markets, among them was Wichita.

The group toured with Cheap Trick and Rick Springfield and began recording a second album. However, being on the road was tiring and the stress soon took its toll on the band. Threet left the band in 1983, with Garry Wall coming on board as guitarist. The following year, the band broke up, its members going on to other careers.

The Crayons

Courtesy: Ron Schauf

At first performing in Dale Stuke's garage, the Crayons played their first gig at Joyland in 1981. The group featured Kenny Haug, guitar and keyboard; Dale Stuke, bass and vocals; Kathy Schauf, vocals and guitar; Ron Schauf, rhythm guitar; and Doug Nelson, drums. The band played The Beer Mill, as well as gigs from the Red Dog saloon to Pratt County Community College for several years.

In 1983, the several members of the Crayons changed the group's name to Dime Novel and included several female musicians. The line up included Kathy Schauf, vocals and drums; Ron Schauf, guitar; Gayle Gilbert-Rhodes, keyboards and vocals; Jane Munro, bass, Georgann Cole, vocals. By this time, however, family and other concerns were becoming important to the band members and the band separated.

Photos courtesy: Harry Dobbin

The FunTones

Phil Snow- bass & vocals; Jim Kent- keyboards, guitar, sax & vocals; John Dondlinger- drums; Harry Dobbin- guitar & vocals; .

A group that consisted of professional musicians that came off the road and attended to real life in Wichita. But they couldn't stop playing music, so they created a local band that played the popular "oldies."

The FunTones became the "party band" for clubs, parties, weddings and plenty of concerts. They were active in a lot of local clubs like the Brickyard, the Blue Note, the Marriott Legend, Wright Bros, Philly Bobs, Margaritas, Bogeys, County Line, Johnny Rockets, Coyote Club and Scatz.

They played frequently for the Wichita River Festival, including the Street Dance and the Oldies Concerts at the West Bank Stage. They also worked with KEYN for many concerts at the Cotillion Ballroom.

Some of the headliners they warmed up for were: Paul Revere and the Raiders, Peter Noone (Herman's Hermits), The Grass Roots,

Johnny Rivers, Mitch Ryder, the Little River Band, Gary Puckett, Mark Lindsey, Chuck Negron and many more.

This band lasted nearly three decades, starting about 1986. There were a couple years that it fell apart but rejoined and kept playing, though the drummers needed to be changed as the years went by. Steve Braswell played for a few years, and then Jim Wood came in until the band broke up in 2016.

Courtesy: Ron Schauf

Badger

In 1979, Ron Schauf went to California under the third incarnation of Shine but when that did not work out, he returned to Wichita, where he became part of Badger.

That group included Ralph Teran, guitar, piano and vocals; Ron Schauf, bass; Gary Fesler, guitar and vocals; Brad Carpenter, drums and vocals. They played at L. Michael's, Foundry Downtown; Foundry West, and other locations before breaking up in 1981.

Walter Ego

Founded by Charlie Cogan and Ron Starkel, Walter Ego was one of Wichita's early New Wave bands. The group played in Wichita from 1980-1982 at venues including The Foundry, Rockpile, and The Cedar.

Featuring Ron Starkel, guitar, bass & vocals; Charlie Cogan, guitar & vocals; Randall Charters, bass & vocals; Vonda Martin, keyboards, bass & vocals; Fred Hamon, drums; Ron Smith, guitar, bass & vocals. Walter Ego played covers by bands such as Rockpile, Elvis Costello, Split Enz, David Bowie, The Stones, Pretenders, and the Kinks.

Band-O-Matic

Formed in 1981, this band consisted of Clay Emberson on lead guitar, Stephen "Rock Stud" Williams on bass and main vocals, Vonda Martin, keyboard and vocals, and Lloyd Miller on drums. This band focused more on the emerging pop music sound of Squeeze, Huey Lewis and The News, and the Originals. Playing in the era of what Emberson recalled as "skinny tie music," the group lasted to about 1983.

Fabulous Shi(r)theads

Formed in 1982, the original concept of the band was to play 1960s music with a "punk attitude." The band made up for their lack of musicianship with attitude and the versatility of their horn section. The film "The Big Chill" came out during that time and allowed people to discover or rediscover '60s R&B and Soul.

The initial nucleus consisted of Dave Clothier on "stun guitar" and lead vocals; Randy Rathbun, guitar, keys and vocals; Clay "Bad Dad" Bastian, saxes and vocals; George Van Riper; trumpet, Larry Beck on bass and Mick Haugen, drums and vocals. Later on, the lineup shifted to include Alan Banta, guitar, lead vocals; Clark Engbrecht, who joined in 1986 on trumpet, keyboards, vocals; and Mike "Mad Dog" Fleming on bass and vocals, who joined in 1987. Joe Worrel joined in 2012 on bass & vocals, Tyler Gauldin on sax and vocals in 2014, Randy Clements on trombone and vocals in 2015 and Bob Kendrick; keys & vocals in 2016.

When it came to the name, Dave Clothier said it was by accident. "When I came back to Wichita, I decided to find some musicians to jam with. I got together with a high school acquaintance and one of his friends who just got out of rehab. I had to teach them the same three chord songs, like Louie, Louie, every time we got together. It was frustrating, and when I was at lunch one day with John Carnes (geologist/guitarist) I told him about my "band". He asked what the name was, and I said "The Fabulous Shitheads." John introduced the band as the Fabulous Shitheads when we got up and played at a Keg Party. The name stuck, and seemed to have a lot do with the band's popularity. People were ready to have fun when they went to see a band with a name like that."

Photos courtesy: Relayer

Relayer

Relayer existed from about 1978 to 1982 and consisted of Michael Gleason, on keyboards, Glenn Salter on guitar, Randy Fields on bass and David Chanowski on drums. They played at venues including Pogo's at Twin Lakes, where they played for T-95's rock & roll night and opened for Chubby Checker. Later Kevin Brown joined on guitar and Steve White on bass.

They had recorded demos at Hi-Fi Studios in Wichita's Riverside neighborhood; The Gaither Studios in Anderson, Indiana, and the Miller studio in Newton with Larry Funk engineering. Mike had been a music theory student at Wichita State and received a call from Kerry Livgren of Kansas asking if he was interested in auditioning for Kansas when Steve Walsh left. Mike later toured with Kansas for their Drastic Measures tour and never looked back.

The Del Reys

Photos courtesy: Kevin May

Steeped in jump blues, rockabilly and soul music, the Del Reys made a name playing predominately in Kansas City, Wichita and the surrounding area. The band's primary transportation was a 1957 purple Chevy station wagon with a Del Reys license plate. During its nearly two-decade existence, the Del Reys became a virtual revolving door of the area's finest musicians.

In 1986, the band entered Jon Miller's studio in Newton to record of an album of obscure blues and rockabilly of the early '50s. The lineup for those sessions, and main core of the band for many years, included Clif Major, lead guitar, vocals; Tommy Crabb, vocals and drums; Rene' Aaron, vocals, harmonica and guitar; Kevin May, saxophone; and Michael Ball, bass. The 12-song album, produced by Larry Funk, featured three Clif Major originals and garnered a five-star review in Guitar Player magazine shortly after its release.

For Major, the Del Reys offered a long overdue return to the electric guitar, after several years of focusing on acoustic music. Fashion was important to the Del Reys and they wore white dinner jackets for wedding gigs, or 1950s cool-cat jackets or cowboy boots and gabardine shirts for regular appearances.

The Del Reys opened for Bo Diddley, JJ Cale, the Thunderbirds, Ronnie Earl and the Broadcasters, Johnny Reno and the Sax Maniacs, and the Paladins. On most nights the band could be found playing at the Spot (an old pool hall on east Douglas), Sister Jenny's in Boulevard Plaza or the Coyote Club on north Broadway. The group also did a stint as house band in the basement of the Holiday Inn on north Broadway, as well as a year playing at the El Dorado Dinner Theater.

As best anyone can recall, the original lineup was comprised of Clif Major, guitar; Jim Kent, vocals, keyboards and saxophone; George Graybill, bass; and Jeff Boaz, drums.

Over the years, the group's membership included such musicians as Kathy Roush Major, Daryl Hawkins, Eric Cale, Gene Bonjiorni, Matt Wilson, Bill Hawks, Mike Ehrke, and Keith Crowell.

The band ended its run around 2004. Clif Major was inducted into the Kansas Music Hall of Fame in 2014.

Straitjack

Courtesy: Straightjack

The band was formed in 1981, consisting entirely of members of the U.S. Air Force stationed at Mcconnell Air Force Base. Though there were a few personnel changes over the years, the majority of time consisted of Jay Cape on lead vocals, Al Lang & Jeff Carron on guitars, Jason Reynolds on bass, Mark Walker on keyboards, and Mick Graham on drums.

Playing off the bad boy image, Straitjack started as a cover band, playing the likes of the Doors, the Who, Van Halen, Aerosmith, & the Ramones to name a few. As the years went by, they began writing their own material, their most recognizable being "One Way Ticket To Nowhere", which was featured on the *Doo Dah* CD from Lace Productions.

Straitjack won several local radio sponsored Battle Of The Bands contests, and were a featured guest of T-95's "15 Minutes Of Fame." They opened for several big-named acts, including the Smithereens and Rick Derringer. Among other merits, they were selected as a local favorite in the Wichita Eagle's Reader's Choice Poll.

The Benders

Courtesy: Kevin May

The Benders first formed in October, 1985. They consist of Byron Brewer, drums and vocals; Larry "Campy" Campanello, bass and vocals; Kevin May, saxophone and vocals; and Johnny Cruz on guitar and vocals. A polished and professional "oldies" band kept the "show" in "showbiz" - with stylish clothes and wild hairdos.

The name "Benders" was used after learning about possibly the first Kansas serial killers. As the legend goes, the Benders invited travelers into their home and then murdered them. A gruesome name.

They have played all over the region and as of this writing continue to draw a good crowd. Bringing their infectious humor and very unique brand of '50s and '60s music, humor and pompadour hairstyles to midwestern stages have kept them constantly busy. At one point, the board members of the Kansas Fairs and Festivals Association declared them the "Number One Fair and Festival Band" in the state, due to the band's overwhelming popularity in this market. They were inducted into the Kansas Music Hall of Fame in 2015.

Sitting Ducks

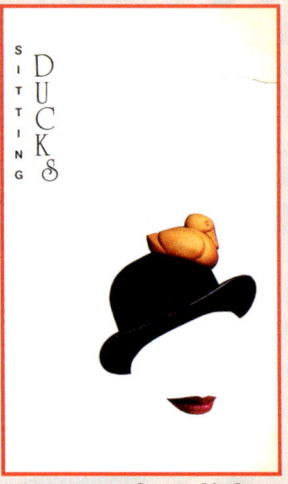
Courtesy: John Stewart

Performing from 1980 through 1985, the Sitting Ducks consisted a number of members who played at various points in the band's career. Among them were Vicki Childers, guitar and vocals; Mark Dannar, guitar; Elaine (Henry) Dannar, guitar and vocals; John Stewart, bass and vocals; Terry Weatherson, drums and vocals; and Gary West, drums and vocals. The Sitting Ducks covered material by groups as varied as the Cars, Paul Revere & the Raiders, the Ventures, the Stray Cats, Robert Gordon, and others. The Sitting Ducks recorded one EP of original material which was scrapped due to a lineup change the week after the recording, and another EP of originals for a person who was interested in possibly managing the band. Neither was released. By the late 1980s, several members moved on to more folk-rock and country groups including Dusty Rose, Mixed Company, and Full House.

Courtesy: Jim Quincy

Dr. Ruth & Good Sax

A riff on the popular book Dr. Ruth's Guide to Good Sex, this 1980s band played rock classics in the local club scene as well as events like Riverfest and Augusta's White Eagle Festival. It consisted initially of Rick Ekum on guitar, Eric Winn on vocals and sax; Jim Quincy on bass; John Ortiz drums; Gail Gilbert keyboards and Georgeanne Cole on vocals. Over the years, the band underwent a number of shifts. Johnny "Patches" Franks replaced Ortiz and married keyboardist Gail Gilbert. When Ekum left, David May became the main guitarist and when May left, Clay Emberson took the role. When Georgeanne left the band, Karen Kirby Kinespel took over on vocals.

Fuzzy Dice

By the early 1980s, several musicians who had known each other through Gandalf and Lickety Split had formed a group called Fuzzy Dice. The band consisted of John Corkum on vocals, Gary Wall on lead guitar; Chris Hutchens on guitar; Steve "Rock Stud" Williams on bass; Woody Schrader on drums. Playing in a pop genre, the band was especially active at Ceasar's Palace.

Courtesy: Klyde Konnor

Klyde Konnor and Tangle Brains

In 1984, a group of high school friends from Norwich, Kansas, came together to form a band. The original lineup was Tim Heuback, John Raida and John Coykendall. In 1985, Coykendall mailed a cassette of home recordings to the KMUW After Midnight program. The name written on the cassette was Klyde Konnor and this, for a time, became the band's name. Coykendall recalled that "the name was a re-spelling of a neighbor's name who always came over to ask them to stop playing. An agreement was arrived at where they could play on Saturday afternoons from 1 until 4 p.m. This was when the wife had her hair done. So, it was on those afternoons that Klyde tracked the louder parts of the initial band recordings." Klyde Konnor consisted initially of Mike Coykendall, drums, guitar, vocals; John Raida, bass and vocals; Tim Heuback, guitar and bass. Known as a "three piece prariepsych band," Klyde Konnor recorded a single "What's She Doin' with Him" in 1985 and, the following year, a full length cassette release titled *The Weaker the Stronger*. Later on, Heuback left and Ron Smith performed bass and vocals and Cameron Gourley on drums and vocals.

Playing music that ranged from The Beatles to Pink Floyd, they performed at Kirby's Beer Store, Coyote Club, The Spot, The B-1 Club, The Flicker, KMUW After Midnight Bashes, Woody's Back Door, and Mile High Club, even getting the title "best band in Kansas" by the Wichita Eagle and Beacon in 1986. In 1987, they released the album *I Always Forget*, one that as more of a safe, pop sound. In response, Klyde began performing more outlandish concerns, earning the group the title "worst live band" in 1988 by the Gopher Purge music magazine. The group continued to record, including the albums *Wallpaper* and *Hypnopatamus*. They also released more experimental sounds under the alter-ego of The Tanglebrains including the albums *Wizard of Owlsley*, *Concept from the Onset*, and *Ill-Dumb*. In 1991, Klyde played their last official show and recorded (in one day) *When Worlds Klyde*. Coykendall then re-located to San Francisco where he formed the folk / Americana group The Old Joe Clarks.

Haze

Courtesy: Kevin Brown

Formed in 1985, Haze consisted of John Smith on vocals, Greg Gilpin and Kevin Brown on guitar, David Castleberry and Randy Spaid on drums, and Pat Case on keyboards. Known for playing "music for the time of your life," the band became especially well known locally for playing private parties and weddings for George Brett, and the Beech and Ruffin families, as well as events for Galichia Medical Group and Pizza Hut, among others. Their main venues included the Candle Club, Tommy's, Harry's Safari (now Margaritas), and Charlie Brown. With its height in popularity in the 1990s, the group lasted until 2001.

Legacy

Courtesy: David Fleming

Formed about 1986, Legacy consisted of Tom Wheeler and David Fleming on guitars, Bud Mitchner on bass, and Woody Schrader on drums. Linda Ward, who had encountered Image when that group was on tour in Houston, relocated to Wichita where she played keyboards and was lead singer. Legacy did mainly cover band music from the progressive rock genre, but was known for playing pieces with its own unique sound. This sound caught the attention of Chanel 95, which arranged for Legacy to open for April Wine.

After a few years, the band underwent a number of changes, starting with Fleming leaving to play with Eddie Lone. A few years later, Ward and Mitchner left and a new version was formed that consisted of a now-returned David Fleming joining Tom Wheeler on guitar, Jan Perez on bass, and Schrader on drums. Through the 1990s, Legacy played local clubs and did some touring but the members now had families and careers that prevented them from traveling too much. The group became known for playing shows for Vietnam Veterans and at Riverfest.

Kevin May and the Deaconairs

Courtesy: Kevin May

First formed in 1988, the Deaconairs desired to preserve a style of performance based on the golden age of stage, when saxophonists were known as the Deacons of Swing and tenor sax was king. The Deaconairs' ocean of material are tunes familiar to big band enthusiasts - Moonlight Serenade, Glen Miller's in The Mood, Benny Goodman's Sing, Sing, Sing, with the signature tom-tom stylings of Gene Krupa ably captured by Stewart. The band members were all professional players, with May working nationwide with Roomful of Blues. They included David Keller on guitar/ vocals, drummer/singer Don Stewart, Keyboard player/vocalist Howard O. Bedient and May on saxophone /vocals. Scott Riggs did replace Keller for a while. Though abundant in vocal talent, the band does just as many instrumentals that showcase their individual musicianship. The Deaconairs philosophy comes from the old school of entertainment. "If you look good you will feel good, and if you feel good you'll be good." Their goal was to put out good music.

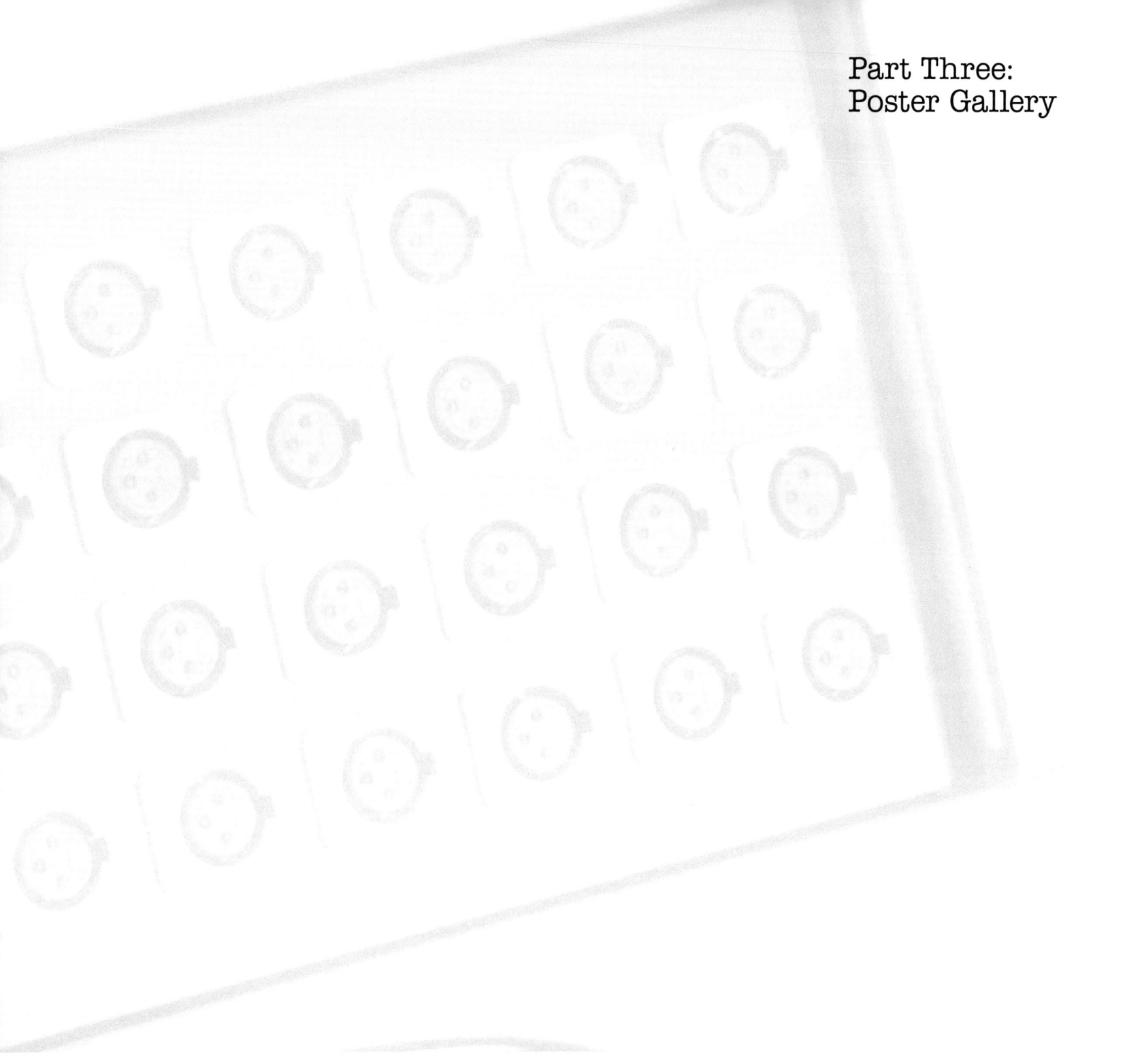

Part Three:
Poster Gallery

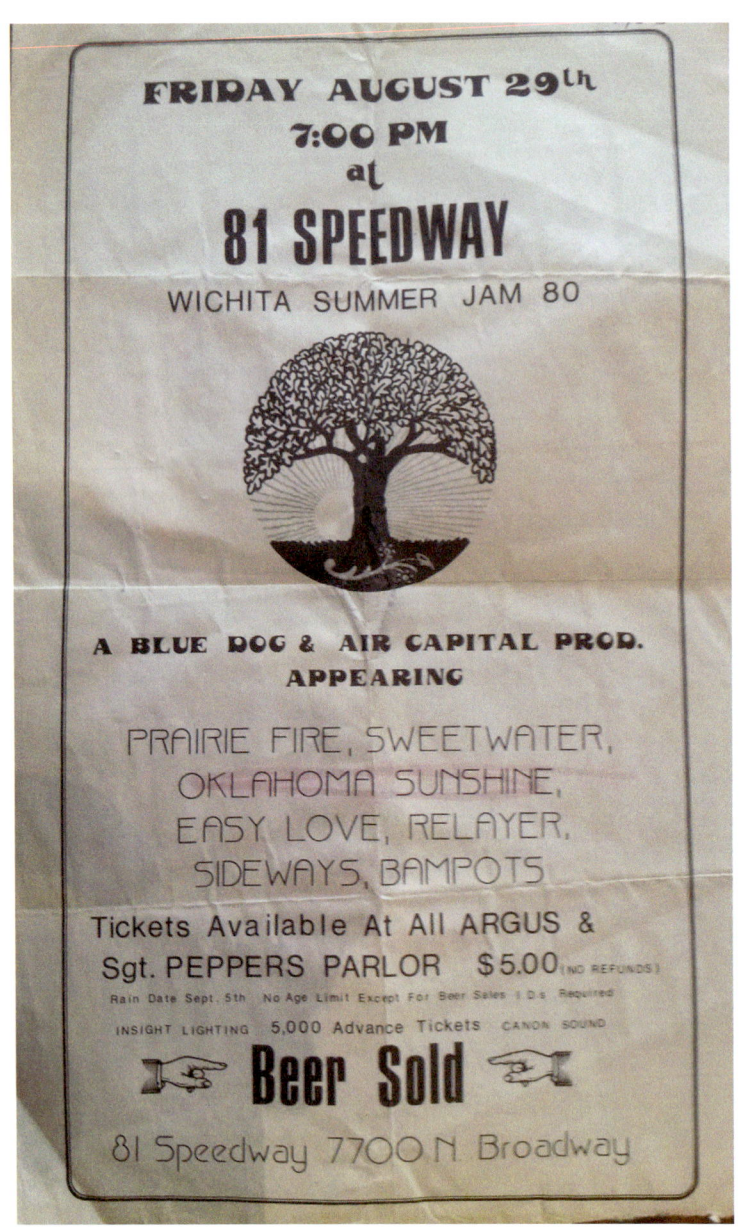

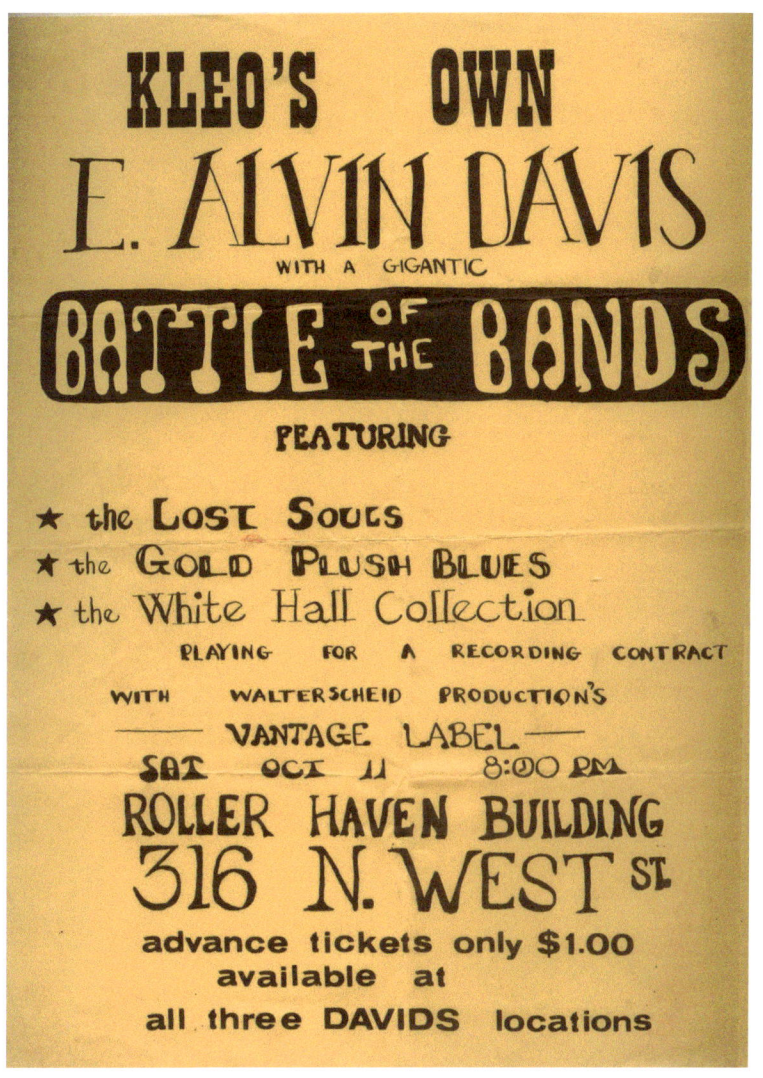

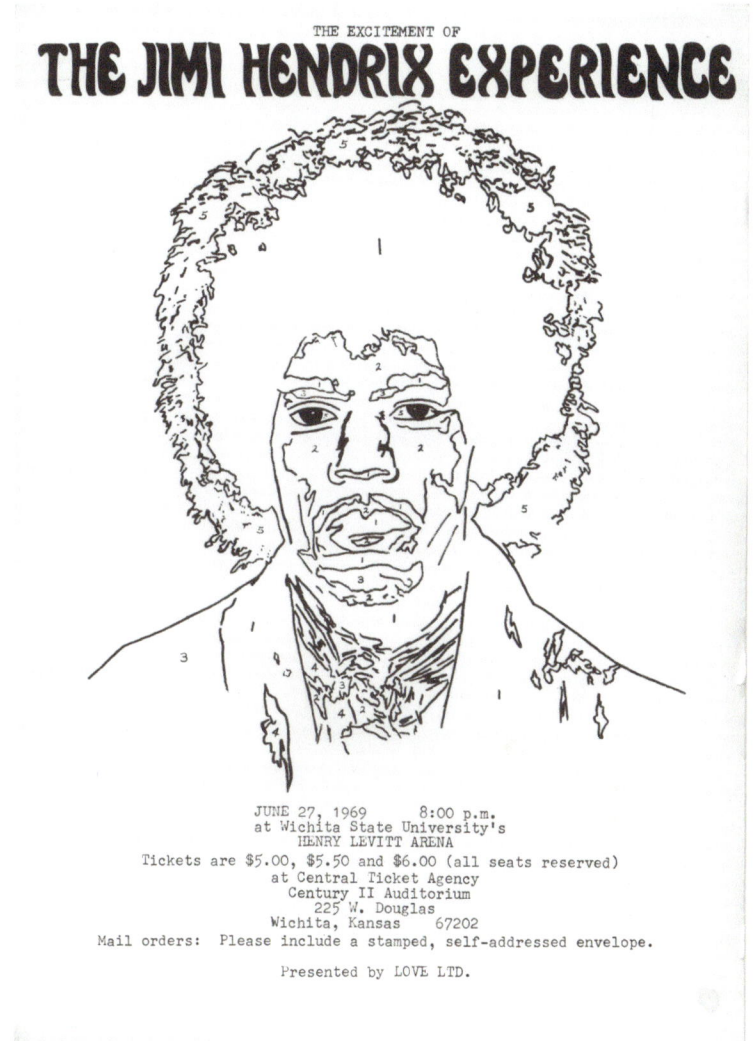

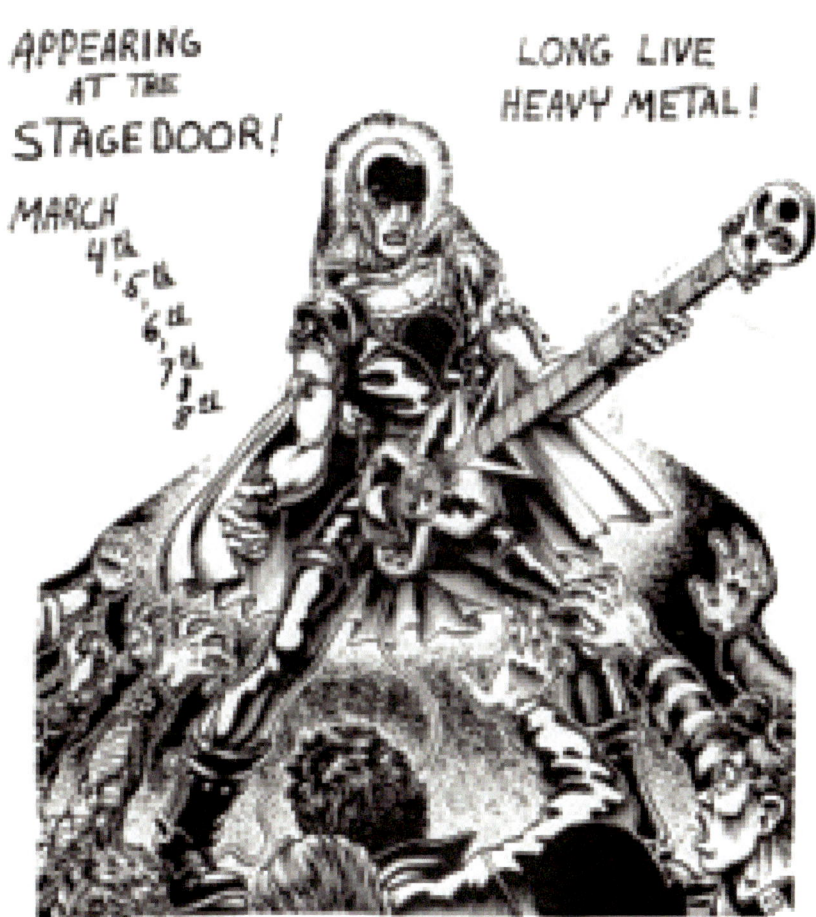

Outdoor Music-Fest '80

Sunday, Aug. 31st

* 2 Miles East of Andover Rd. on Pawnee *
Gates Open at Noon

Five Live Bands
FROM 1 TO 12 PM

Sweet Water The Clocks
Ozone Relayer
Oklahoma Sunshine

"100 Kegs of Free Beer"

MUST BE 18 OR OLDER TO ATTEND
ID'S WILL BE CHECKED

Food and Soft Drinks Available

Admission $6.00
at the gate

Advance Tickets $5.00
50¢ of each ticket goes to support Muscular Dystrophy Association

Available At All:
All Argus Locations
Budget Tapes & Records
Studio 19
Celebrity Tickets

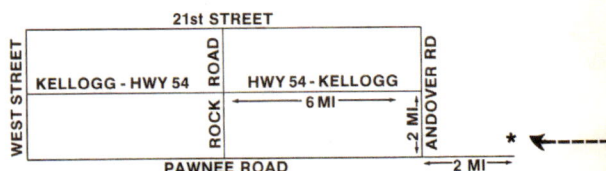

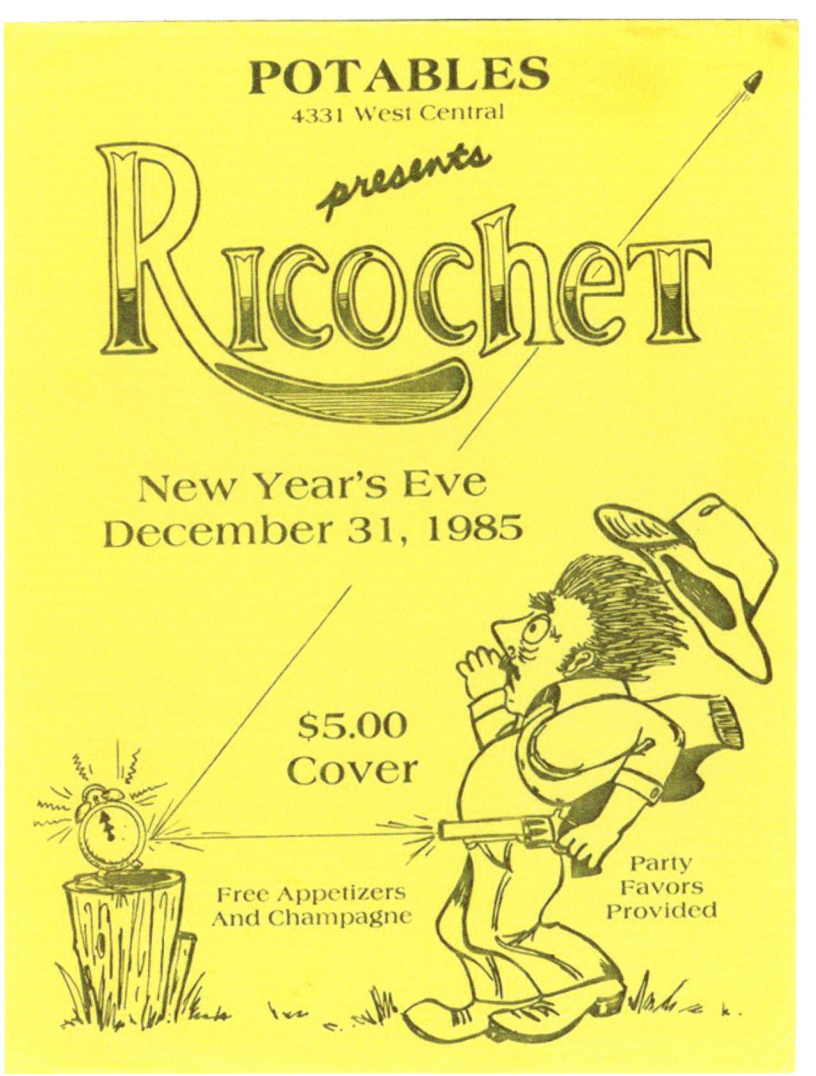

ROCK-N-TONES

at the

Rock Castle

3818 NORTH BROADWAY

Friday & Saturday Nights

12:30 to 3:30 a. m.

(OPEN AT 10 PM)

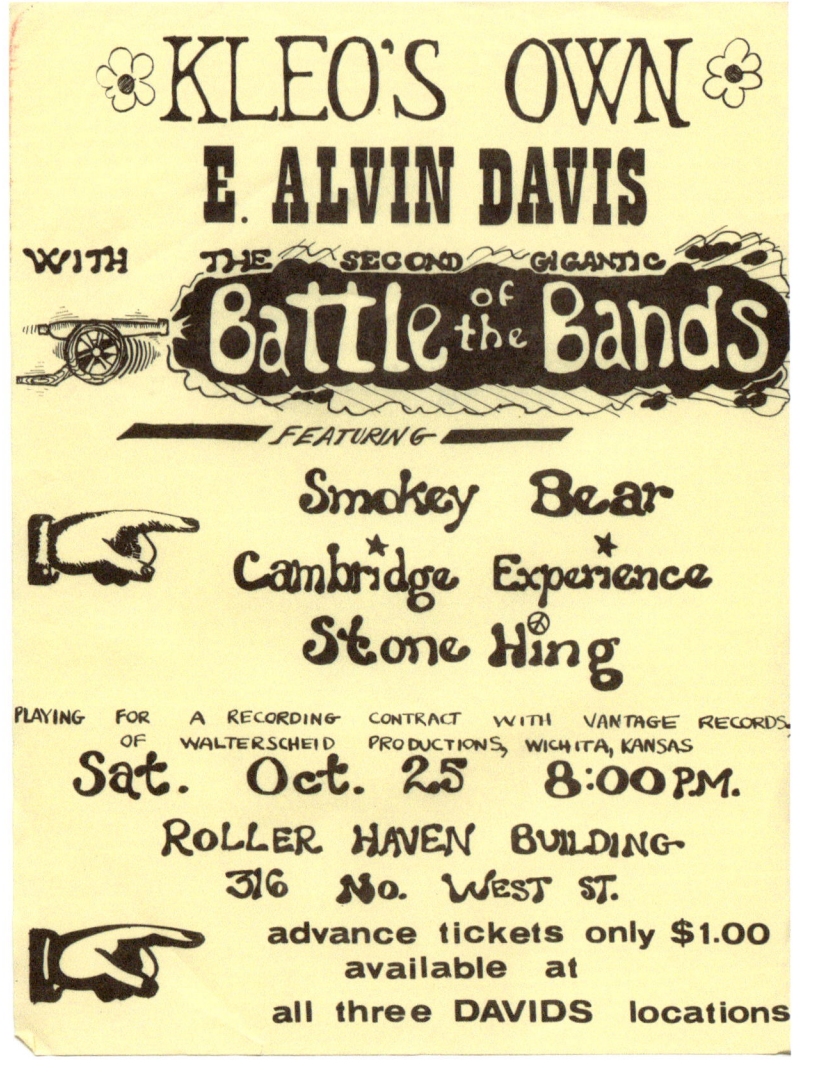

Dr. Rita Rizzi, marine zoologist asks...

"If Dolphins are so *smart*, why don't they ever come out and *BOP* with the *SITTING DUCKS*?"

TEEN AGERS

TEEN CLUB

47th & S. Clifton   Middle of Oaklawn
In Body Shop Bldg.   JA 4-9256

OPEN EVERY SUNDAY

4 to 10 p.m.

TROPHIES AWARDED EVERY SUNDAY

BATTLE of the BANDS

Sound Wave - Smoky Bear

Cambridge Experiment

Whitehall Collection

Admission $1.00

81

TEEN CLUB

8025 S. Broadway

JA 4-9215

OPEN EVERY SUNDAY

4 to 10 p.m.

TROPHIES AWARDED EVERY SUNDAY

Music by Gold Plush Blues

Admission $1.00

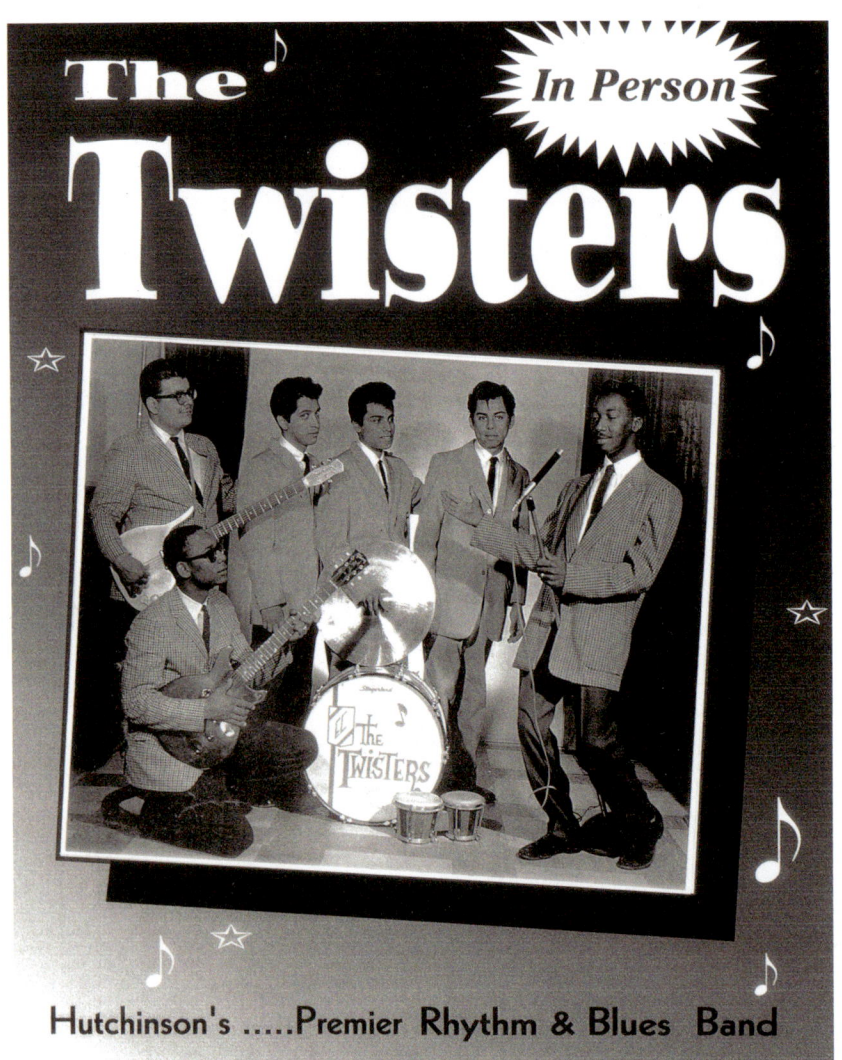